HEALING

Through the

POWER *of*

PRAYER

Timothy J. Dailey, Ph.D.

Publications International, Ltd.

Timothy J. Dailey, Ph.D., earned his doctorate in theology from Marquette University and studied at Wheaton College and the Institute of Holy Land Studies, Jerusalem. He has taught theology, biblical history, and comparative religion in the United States and Israel, including the Biblical Resources Study Center, Jerusalem, and Jerusalem Center for Biblical Studies.

Photo credits:
Front cover: **John Terence Turner/FPG International.**
The Crosiers: Table of contents (right), 77, 148, 154, 164, 175, 206, 226, 238; **FPG International:** William Adams: 112; Kimberley Belfi: 174; Bruce Byers: 87; Ron Chapple: 80; Willard Clay: 7; Robert Cundy: 34; Michael Goldman: 86; Dennis Hallinan: 225, 234; Nancy Hill: 97; H. Richard Johnston: 71, 142; James McLoughlin: 90; Christian Michaels: 120; Yoichiro Miyazaki: 44; E. Nagele: 113; Richard Nowitz: 235; Eberhard Otto: 130; G. Randall: 105; Galen Rowell: 51; Miguel S. Salmeron: 155; Michael Shay: 172; Richard H. Smith: 199; Studio Pierer: 35; Thayer Syme: 207; Bob Taylor: 239; Telegraph Colour Library: 17, 28, 29, 56, 64, 65, 89, 125, 131, 137, 183; Ron Thomas: 123; L. West: 136; **Kathleen Marsh Photography:** Table of contents (left), 8, 9, 25, 50, 57, 76, 91, 121, 124, 143, 149, 157, 173, 181, 209, 214, 215, 220, 221, 227; **Zev Radovan:** 16, 24, 45, 70, 81, 96, 104; **SuperStock:** 156, 165, 180, 184, 185, 190, 191, 198, 208, 232.

ACKNOWLEDGMENTS
The publisher gratefully acknowledges the kind permission granted to reprint the following copyrighted material. Should any copyright holder have been inadvertently omitted, they should apply to the publisher, who will be pleased to credit them in full in any subsequent editions.

Excerpts from *Prayer Is Good Medicine* by Larry Dossey. Copyright © 1996 by Larry Dossey, M.D. Reprinted by permission of HarperCollins Publishers, Inc.

Excerpts from *Healing Words* by Larry Dossey. Copyright © 1993 by Larry Dossey, M.D. Reprinted by permission of HarperCollins Publishers, Inc.

Excerpts from *Forgive and Forget* by Lewis B. Smedes. Copyright © 1984 by Lewis B. Smedes. Reprinted by permission of HarperCollins Publishers, Inc.

Excerpts from *Healing and Christianity* by Morton Kelsey. Copyright © 1995 by Morton Kelsey. Used by permission of Augsburg Fortress.

Excerpts from *The Journey to Wholeness: A Christ-Centered Approach to Health and Healing* by Kenneth L. Bakken and Kathleen H. Hofeller. Copyright © 1988 by Kenneth L. Bakken and Kathleen H. Hofeller. All rights reserved. Used with permission of The Crossroad Publishing Company, New York.

Excerpts from *Channels of Healing Prayer* by Benedict Heron, OSB, Ave Maria Press, 1989, Notre Dame, Indiana. Used by permission.

Excerpts from *The Uncommon Touch* by Tom Harpur. Copyright © 1994 by Tom Harpur. Used by permission of McClelland & Stewart Inc.

Excerpts from *Taken From Heaven, Your Real Home* by Joni Eareckson Tada. Copyright © 1995 by Joni Eareckson Tada. Used by permission of Zondervan Publishing House.

Manufactured in China

8 7 6 5 4 3 2 1

ISBN: 0-7853-2434-8

CONTENTS

INTRODUCTION

*O Lord, you have searched me
and known me. . . . For it was you
who formed my inward parts; you
knit me together in my mother's
womb. I praise you, for I am
fearfully and wonderfully made.*

Psalm 139:1,13

You need only glance at today's headlines to know that people are probing the relationship between healing and prayer. Perhaps the reason these reviews make headlines is that the outcome is unexpected: Studies have shown that patients who are prayed for do better than those who are not.

Healing Through the Power of Prayer presents evidence of God's answers to prayers. The history of healing is recounted, including before and after the Bible was written. Recent anecdotal evidence and evidence offered by the latest scientific studies are also included. They will help build your faith in things you may not yet have experienced, so that you can pray for those who need a miracle.

Scripture verses are included so that you may use them to enrich your faith in God's ability and desire to heal. As you become more grounded in the possibilities of prayer, these verses will become an active part of your prayer life or quiet time. You'll also find chapters to help you examine your life as you pray, to be sure you are walking according to God's will.

The importance of forgiveness is explained, as well as other attributes, so that you may grow and experience God's work in your life. Encouragement, inspiration, and empowerment await you; they are a gift from God.

Part I:

A Brief History of Healing

One man was there who had been ill for thirty-eight years. When Jesus saw him lying there and knew that he had been there a long time, he said to him, "Do you want to be made well?" The sick man answered him, "Sir, I have no one to put me into the pool when the water is stirred up; and while I am making my way, someone else steps down ahead of me." Jesus said to him, "Stand up, take your mat and walk." At once, the man was made well, and he took up his mat and began to walk.

John 5:5-9

Healing Through the Power of Prayer

CHAPTER 1:
The Miracle Kid

Then one of the leaders of the
synagogue named Jairus came and,
when he saw him, fell at his feet and
begged him repeatedly, "My little
daughter is at the point of death.
Come and lay your hands on her, so
that she may be made well, and live."

Mark 5:22–23

When ten-year-old Dierdre Aragon said she wasn't feeling well, her parents, Kathy and Tino, were not unduly worried. They assumed their daughter was coming down with a bad case of the flu. By the next day,  however, their concern changed to alarm when Dierdre's con- dition deteriorated rapidly. She was crying out in pain; she could no longer sit up or focus her eyes. Kathy and Tino rushed her to the emergency room at their local hospital where the doctors examined her and ran tests to determine what was wrong.

It seemed to take forever for the results to come back as they waited anxiously by their daughter's bedside. When Kathy and Tino finally heard the diagnosis they were stunned: Dierdre had contracted Reye syndrome. "The bottom fell out of my world," says Kathy, "I'd read about Reye's and knew it had a high mortality rate."[1]

Dierdre was immediately transferred to the nearby university medical center that was better equipped to handle cases like hers. The surgeons operated, but despite their best efforts, Dierdre's condition deteriorated. She developed pneumonia and slipped into a coma. Hour by hour the days passed as Kathy and Tino maintained a vigil at Dierdre's bedside. Then, on day four of her illness, the doctors informed them that Dierdre had lost all cognitive brain function. All that remained was to await the inevitable. Kathy and Tino were asked to sign a do-not-resuscitate order.

Kathy and Tino were shocked and heartbroken. Almost overnight, their healthy and active daughter had entered into a near-vegetative state—and there was nothing the doctors could do to cure her. It seemed that all was lost.

But the battle was not over yet. As Kathy and Tino tried to prepare themselves for the worst, concerned friends enlisted one last weapon in the fight to save Dierdre: prayer. Word spread, and an around-the-clock prayer vigil was organized. Soon, more than 2,200 people from 16 different congregations were praying for her. The cumulative effect of their petitions was soon felt.

Back at the hospital, Dierdre's doctors waited helplessly for her to die. But she didn't. Instead, as her doctor was

Healing Through the Power of Prayer

examining her, her doctor was surprised to see her pupils responding to light. That was the first indication that the tide had turned. To the doctors' amazement, she began to improve, and a week later her parents and the doctors were astounded to see the child the doctors now called "The Miracle Kid" walking.

A month later, Dierdre returned to school half time. She continued to improve until her recovery was complete. She excelled in school and went on to become an honor student. Her former neurologist, Dr. Lillian Pardo, could only conclude: "This family was determined to get their child back. I think their prayers had an effect."

When confronted with an intractable disease, Dierdre's family and friends did what surveys indicate many others are doing: They prayed for

divine intervention. A Time/CNN poll of 1,004 Americans revealed that 82 percent of the respondents believed in the healing power of prayer. In addition, 62 percent thought that doctors should be willing to pray for their patients.

Sound surprising? A growing body of evidence shows that prayer indeed works. On the following pages some extraordinary reports of miraculous healings—dating from the earliest days of the Church to the present—will be examined. And those accounts will be buttressed with scientific evidence demonstrating that religious faith and prayer can actually help bring about healing.

So why aren't more physicians praying with their patients? According to Dr. David Larson of the National Institute for Healthcare Research, the reason is that they have no one to pray to: Surveys report that fewer than two thirds of all doctors believe in God. That puts many in the healing professions out of touch with the spiritual needs of those they serve. As Larson says: "We physicians are culturally insensitive about the role of religion. It is very important to many of our patients and not important to lots of doctors."[2]

All this indicates that our medical system needs to be revised to better allow for the spiritual needs of patients. Larson believes, for example, that hospital patients have the right to be asked a few simple questions, such as whether their religion is important to them and, if so, would they like to be prayed for by the hospital chaplain or another member of the clergy? To fail to do this, according to Larson, is to do a disservice to their patients.

Some, like Dr. James Krahn, are already putting Larson's recommendations into practice. The Winnipeg physician makes prayer a regular part of his medical practice. When he examines his patients, he calls upon the assistance of the Great Physician: "With my hands on their shoulder I listen to their breathing and I silently pray for their healing."[3]

Dr. Krahn became interested in the subject after reviewing scientific studies showing that patients who are prayed for recover more quickly than those who are not. Praying for healing was ignored when he was in medical school. One report that

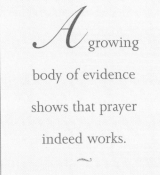

A growing body of evidence shows that prayer indeed works.

impressed him surveyed more than 130 studies on prayer. It concluded that prayer had a positive effect upon a variety of illnesses, including high blood pressure, asthma, and heart attacks.

Krahn is convinced that praying for healing works. He believes that doctors should seek divine assistance for their patients as a regular part of their practice: "It is an essential and complementary part of the therapeutic approach, along with medication and surgery," he says. "Doctors would be in denial to discount the value of prayer."[4]

Not all would agree. Skeptics scoff at such reports, insisting that answers to prayer are nothing more than the power of suggestion. A group called the Committee for the Scientific Investigation of Paranormal Claims puts prayer in the same class of dubious claims as spoon bending. They insist that so-called physical healings occur only in the mind—whether conscious or subconscious. The individuals may convince themselves that they are "healed"; they may even see some temporary improvement in their condition. But sooner or later their symptoms will reappear.

It cannot be denied that there is a measure of truth to this

> *K*rahn is convinced that praying for healing works. He believes that doctors should seek divine assistance for their patients as a regular part of their practice.

view. Some faith healers have been known to employ questionable methods; they have manipulated their followers into believing they have been healed. In his book *The Uncommon Touch*, Tom Harpur discusses the ministry of one colorful evangelist and relates an incident he witnessed: "Certainly there are humorous moments. . . . I remember once covering a crusade of his at the International Centre, near the Toronto airport, where a man who said he was deaf in one ear came forward for healing. [The evangelist] had the man indicate which ear was the problem. Then, shouting 'Jeeeeezues heal!' he clapped both his hands over the man's ears with considerable force. Though he only whispered it, the microphone picked up and amplified the man's voice as he blurted, 'Oh my God, there goes my good ear!'"[5]

Harpur, a hard-bitten journalist and religion editor, has observed every trick in the book at healing crusades. The presence of rented wheelchairs in the lobby of the auditorium is one sure giveaway. People who are physically challenged generally do not expect wheelchairs to be provided for them—they usually take their own wheelchairs with them wherever they go. Harpur has seen people who were perfectly able to walk sit in the rented wheelchairs and then jump up and run down the aisles for the cameras, creating the false impression of people who could not walk being healed.

Harpur reserves his harshest criticism for those who shamelessly extort money from their followers. Despite his cynicism regarding the abuses of some faith healers, Harpur makes a cogent observation: "It is too easy simply to write off healers and healing because of the gross conduct of certain so-called faith healers. . . . The misuse of something in no way establishes a case against its proper use,"[6] any more than medical malpractice should be allowed to serve as an indictment of the entire medical profession.

Harpur is correct here: The existence of fraud does not negate the real thing. One might be able to show the falsity of some—even many—alleged healings, but to deny outright the possibility of healing is a self-defeating endeavor. It is not likely to take any open-minded investigator very long to discover a few cases where the sicknesses or injuries actually disappeared.

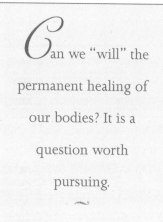

Can we "will" the permanent healing of our bodies? It is a question worth pursuing.

What about such instances of healing that cannot be explained away? Harpur admits that "as a journalist I long ago became aware that sometimes, in spite of all the froth and all the manipulation, there are people who are transformed inwardly and healed outwardly as a result of encountering one of these showmen."[7]

His innate journalistic skepticism notwithstanding, Harpur concedes that he has observed what appeared to be healings. Is it possible he is mistaken? Can recoveries like that of Dierdre Aragon be explained by the power of suggestion—can we "will" the permanent healing of our bodies? It is a question worth pursuing.

Healing Through the Power of Prayer

THE MIND-BODY CONNECTION

Medical research is only beginning to discover ways in which the mind influences the body. For example, a person's thoughts can trigger stress hormones that affect the immune system. The same thing can happen with a placebo (a "sugar pill" that has no medicinal properties). Placebos have accounted for some remarkable—if temporary—physical improvements. Some studies have shown that hospital patients can experience pain relief when they think that the sugar pill they are taking is actually a powerful painkiller.

In their book *The Power of the Mind to Heal*, the husband-wife physician team of Joan and Miroslav Borysenko document the humorous lengths to which the mind can influence the body: "In one fascinating study, a third of the women who got placebo chemotherapy treat-ments in a clinical trial testing the efficacy of the drug actually lost their hair!"[8] These hapless women mistakenly thought they were receiving chemotherapy and dutifully lost their hair like all chemo patients should. In another study devised by some mischievous doctors, pregnant women who suffered from severe morning sickness were given syrup of ipecac, a potent drug used to induce vomiting. The women were told that the drug would settle their stomachs, and sure enough, in over half of them it did.

THE CASE OF THE "MIRACLE DRUG" KREBIOZEN

A more serious example of the power of auto-suggestion was reported years ago in the *Journal of Prospective Techniques*. In the article entitled "Psychological Variables in Human Cancer," Psychologist Bruno Klopfer

Healing Through the Power of Prayer

describes the case of a man in the advanced stages of cancer of the lymph nodes. This particularly vicious form of cancer had spread throughout the patient's body, and he was expected to die within a few weeks. He was bedridden and could breath only with great difficulty.

The man heard about a new experimental drug called Krebiozen, which reportedly had been shown to be effective against lymphatic cancer. Despite his precarious condition, the man insisted on being prescribed a clinical trial of the drug, believing it was his only hope. His doctors relented and gave him an injection of Krebiozen.

In no time at all, the man appeared to make a miraculous  recovery, astounding his doctors. Tests revealed that his tumors had completely disappeared, and in ten days he was discharged from the hospital. He presented every appearance of being in good health and was able to resume much of his normal routine.

After about two months, however, news reports began to circulate questioning the effectiveness of Krebiozen. After he learned of these reports, the man's symptoms soon reappeared, and he was readmitted to the hospital. Tests revealed that the man's tumors had returned.

His physician, realizing that the man's condition was critical, decided on a desperate gamble. He explained to the man that the original batches of Krebiozen had deteriorated with storage. However, a new and more potent version was now available that he was prepared to administer to the patient.

Healing Through the Power of Prayer

The doctor then proceeded to inject him with what amounted to nothing more than purified water. Nevertheless, the effect was again extraordinary. The patient experienced a dramatic remission; his tumors shrank, and he left the hospital.

After several months, however, the American Medical Association completed a nationwide study on the effectiveness of the drug, followed by newspaper headlines announcing: "Nationwide AMA tests show Krebiozen to be worthless as a cancer treatment." This news had a devastating effect upon the man, who died less than two days later.[9]

Do tragic cases like these explain what happens when people say they have been "healed"? Is it just a temporary case of mind over matter? Some say it is, especially with regard to phenomena like the highly charged atmosphere of faith healing meetings and the heightened expectations that accompany the laying on of hands. Such people, they claim, get caught up in an emotional experience and somehow manage to convince themselves that they have been healed. For a period of time, they may even

> *In no time at all, the man appeared to make a miraculous recovery, astounding his doctors. Tests revealed that his tumors had completely disappeared.*

Healing Through the Power of Prayer

feel better and note some improvement in their condition.

The opposite can also be true: People can "will" sickness or even death upon themselves, as demonstrated by the unfortunate story told by Dr. Bernard Lown, professor of cardiology at Harvard University. Lown was in the hospital visiting with a patient when the chief of staff and several other medical students came into the room. They examined his patient, a middle-aged woman with congestive heart failure and swelling in the ankles. The woman's condition was not so serious that she could not continue her work as a librarian and live a relatively normal life.

If you have faith the size of a mustard seed . . . nothing will be impossible for you.

Matthew 17:20

After his examination, the chief of staff turned to his students and in the woman's presence announced: "This woman has TS." Without explaining the term to her, the doctor and his students then moved on to the next patient, leaving the woman in a state of confusion about what he had meant.

The patient's condition began to disintegrate almost immediately. She began breathing rapidly, and her pulse rate shot up dramatically.

Upon examining her, Lown found that fluid was accumulating in her lungs. He asked her what was wrong. The woman replied that the doctor had just told her that she had TS, which she took to mean "terminal situation." Lown hastened to explain to her that this is not what TS means. It is actually the abbreviation for tricuspid stenosis—the narrowing of the tricuspid heart valve—which is not in itself terminal.

The woman would have none of it. She remained convinced that her condition was hopeless. Later that day, she died from massive lung congestion and heart failure.[10]

Most of us are familiar with the risk factors for heart disease, the number one cause of death in the United States. These include hypertension, high cholesterol, obesity, smoking, and a sedentary lifestyle. However, this is not the whole story, as Drs. Joan and Miroslav Borysenko explain: "But did you know that the majority of first heart attacks aren't related to any of these major risk factors? What do you think they *are* related to? Well, here's a hint.

The majority of initial heart attacks occur on a Monday and are clustered between 8:00 and 9:00 A.M.! Some companies call this the 'parking lot syndrome.' A Massachusetts study found that these Monday morning heart attacks were actually related to two key psychological factors: job dissatisfaction and lack of joy." [11]

There can be little doubt that for better or worse our mental perceptions can influence our bodies. This can be true for people whose fears and unhappiness cause illness and even death. It can also be true for those who desperately want to believe that they are healed. But this is not always the case: There are many whose healings cannot be attributed to auto-suggestion. This is because any positive effects of auto-suggestion are rarely permanent, as Blair Justice, Ph.D., writes in his book *Who Gets Sick: How Beliefs, Moods, and*

Thoughts Affect Your Health: "The internal healing systems that apparently can be turned on by a profound belief in something have repeatedly demonstrated their power, but they rarely can reverse a case of advanced cancer. They may slow the disease or facilitate a remission, but there is little evidence that they 'cure.'"[12]

Cases where the healing is not temporary and the patient remains cured cannot easily be attributed to the power of auto-suggestion. This is the conclusion of researcher David J. Hufford, Ph.D., of Penn State University. Hufford is convinced there is more to many healings than auto-suggestion.

One case in particular impressed him. Sally was born with sickle-cell anemia, an incurable blood disease that typically causes fatigue, headaches, and shortness of breath. More seriously, it can also lead to sickle-cell crises that, explains Dr. Hufford, "are extremely painful, reduce life expectancy and can be fatal."

Sally attended a healing service at which she believed she was cured. The change was dramatic: "She no longer became breathless or tired," said Dr. Hufford. "In fact she was even able to take a door-to-door selling job, something she couldn't have done before." Although Sally still tests positive for sickle-cell anemia, in over 20 years she has remained healthy and has outlived her doctor's expectations.

> *There can be little doubt that for better or worse our mental perceptions can influence our bodies.*

Healing Through the Power of Prayer

Says Dr. Hufford: "It looks to me like a miracle. It's probably not great for me professionally to be saying this, and for those who don't want to believe, there's still the mind-body explanation. But I think that to attribute it to the placebo effect is a cop-out."[13]

It might be possible to mask the symptoms of a disease for a few weeks or months. But 20 years is a long time. It is highly unlikely that Sally has managed to deceive herself for so many years. The most reasonable explanation is that she has indeed experienced a genuine—though not complete—healing.

Other research has been specifically designed to test the auto-suggestion hypothesis. In one such study, for example, sick babies who were prayed for by healers showed positive improvement in comparison to a control group of infants who did not receive prayer. The infants were obviously incapable of responding to any power of suggestion.

In yet another study that became the subject of a BBC documentary entitled "A Way of Healing," 44 volunteers received identical skin-deep wounds. In a rigidly controlled experiment, one half of the group was prayed for by a healer without their knowledge. They healed much better than the control group, who were not prayed for. The 13 who were prayed for were further along in the healing process; each had a layer of new tissue over each wound. The other group, which was not prayed for, had no closed wounds.[14]

The researchers were careful to prevent any possibility of auto-suggestion. In fact, the true purpose of the study was such a closely guarded fact that not only the volunteers but also the project manager were totally unaware that it was designed to test the effectiveness of prayer. This eliminated the possibility that those administering the tests could convey any expectations to the participants.

This experimental evidence demonstrates that prayer can bring about healing in circumstances where auto-suggestion or positive thinking is not a factor. Of course, any such evidence is unlikely to convince the die-hard skeptic. The maxim "there are none so blind as those who will not see" is especially appropriate when it comes to the healing power of prayer.

We should not underestimate our capacity for self-delusion and denial. In his classic work *Healing and Christianity*, Morton Kelsey describes a revealing experiment devised by psychologists at Harvard University: "[The researchers] took a black six of spades from a deck of playing cards and had it painted red. The card was reinserted in the deck and shown to a large number of subjects. Practically none of them reported the card as a red six of spades. They reported seeing either a black six of spades or the six of diamonds or hearts. *What they had no place for in their belief system they actually did not see.* The failure to see what one rationally should perceive is called cognitive dissonance."[15]

> *Why is it that some—even in the Christian community—have little place in their belief system for the reality of healing through prayer?*

When it comes to miraculous healing, self-deception is a two-edged sword. Certainly there are those unfortunate souls who mistakenly believe they have been healed. But there are also those who are equally unfortunate in their adamant refusal to consider the possibility of divine healing.

RELIGIOUS FAITH AND HEALTH

Why is it that some—even in the Christian community—have little place in their belief system for the reality of healing through prayer? The blame can be laid squarely at the feet of a culture that has largely rejected the possibility of miracles. After all—it is confidently proclaimed—ours is the age of science, not superstition! People in ancient times frequently attributed what they could not explain to spiritual forces. We know better! We understand that nothing occurs outside of the known laws of physics. The so-called "miracles" of times past were merely the reflection of the ignorance of a prescientific age.

For a long time, orthodox medicine mirrored this cultural skepticism. It placed supreme confidence in medical science, dismissing healing through spiritual means as a relic from the Dark Ages. No longer. The secret is out: Religious faith is good for you. As Dr. David B. Larson says, "I was told by my [medical school] professors that religion is harmful. Then I looked at the research, and religion is actually highly beneficial. If you go to church and pray regularly, it's very beneficial in terms of preventing illness, mental and physical, and you cope with illness much more effectively."[16]

Thirty of the 126 medical schools in the country now

have courses in faith and medicine. This seismic change is the result of a growing body of evidence confirming the healing power of prayer. Larson's National Institute for Healthcare Research has examined more than 200 studies on the relationship between religion and health.[17] Many of them show a significant correlation between the two, including the following:

Hypertension: Larson surveyed the past 30 years of research and found that those who attend

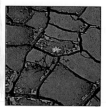

religious ceremonies regularly have lower blood pressure on

average than those who do not. This holds true even when adjusted for other risk factors such as smoking.

Emotional Health: A significant number of studies have demonstrated a relationship between religious faith and emotional health. Religious commitment was associated with lower rates of mental disorder and drug use. If the pressures of life and work are getting you down, try joining the more than 40 percent of Americans who worship on a regular basis. Those who attend church regularly have lower rates of depression and illness resulting from stress. Additionally, 19 out of

> *If the pressures of life and work are getting you down, try joining the more than 40 percent of Americans who worship on a regular basis.*

Healing Through the Power of Prayer

20 studies showed religion playing a positive role in preventing alcoholism.

Conversely, the suicide rate of those who have no religious affiliation is four times that of those who have a strong religious faith. Sixteen out of 17 studies confirmed that religious faith had a positive role in reducing suicide.

The benefits of practicing religious faith continue as we grow older. In 1996, the National Institute on Aging released a study of 4,000 elderly people living at home. The study found that those who go to church or synagogue regularly enjoyed better emotional health and less depression than those who did not. In another study of 30 female patients recovering from hip surgery, those who had a strong religious faith not only suffered less from depression but were able to walk better upon dis-

charge from the hospital.

Cardiovascular Disease: More people die from cardiovascular disease than from any other single cause—and here the positive benefits from prayer and religious faith are nothing short of dramatic. A 1995 study of 232 heart surgery patients at Dartmouth-Hitchcock Medical Center found that those who said they drew comfort and strength from their religious faith had less than one third the death rate of those who did not. Other studies indicate that even when high-risk factors such as smoking are taken into account, men and women who attend church have half the risk of dying from coronary-artery disease than those who do not attend.

In the early 1980s, cardiologist Randolph Byrd conducted

what has become a classic study on the effects of prayer on heart patients. Byrd divided 400 cardiac patients in a coronary care unit at San Francisco General Hospital into two groups. He then recruited both Roman Catholic and Protestant groups to intercede for the first group. They were given the patient's name and condition and asked to pray for them daily. Those in the control group did not receive prayer from the prayer groups.

Byrd conducted a double-blind study, which meant that neither the patients nor their doctors knew which patients were the objects of prayer. This was important to avoid the possibility of auto-suggestion: If the patients knew they were being prayed for they might show superficial improvement. In this case, it would be their minds influencing their bodies, not prayer. It was important to ensure they were not aware they were being prayed for.

Byrd found that the patients who were prayed for did better than the control group. They were less likely to develop congestive heart failure, they had fewer complications, and they were five times less likely to require antibiotics.

All this constitutes an impressive body of scientific evidence

> *Why are those who pray for healing in many cases not healed, while the irreligious sometimes appear to sail right through life enjoying good health?*

demonstrating the healing power of prayer. This is not to say that those of strong religious faith will enjoy perpetual health—or vice versa. God's ways are too mysterious for that, as is evidenced by the curious phenomenon of the "healthy reprobate." History is replete with examples of those who lived to a ripe old age all the while thumbing their nose at traditional religion.

Celebrated playwright and skeptic George Bernard Shaw lived a long and healthy life despite his rejection of organized Christianity. He finally succumbed to injuries sustained in a fall after climbing an apple tree on a dare at the advanced age of 94. The outspoken atheist Bertrand Russell died peacefully at the advanced age of 97.

When we compare such men with those who in spite of their devout faith succumb to disease at an early age, it seems unfair. Why are those who pray for healing in many cases not healed, while the irreligious sometimes appear to sail right through life enjoying good health? We are not always able to understand God's reasonings.

Healing Through the Power of Prayer

CHAPTER 2:
Let This Tumor Wither!

> "I have heard your prayer,
> I have seen your tears; indeed,
> I will heal you."
>
> 2 Kings 20:5

"I'm afraid I have bad news," began the call on December 12, 1994. Joy Sandifer sank down into her family-room sofa, her heart racing. Her doctor continued, "I just got the lab results back. You have a three-centimeter tumor in your intestine. We need to operate as soon as possible." The doctor wanted to operate two days

later—on Wednesday—but agreed to wait until Friday.

Three-centimeter tumor! Appalled, Sandifer hung up the phone and gazed down at her distended stomach. She knew something was very wrong: She hadn't felt right for quite a while. But she had desperately hoped for a more benign explanation. Such a verdict would hit anyone like a bomb-shell. It meant major surgery to remove the tumor along with several inches of intestine. But for 48-year-old Joy Sandifer it was a virtual death sentence— she no longer had several inches of her intestine to spare.

Up until several years ago, Sandifer, a fit and trim house-wife and mother, had scarcely been sick a day in her life. Her first bout with intestinal prob-lems began unexpectedly one afternoon at a local mall. She was waiting at a snack bar for her husband Jim to finish his Christmas shopping.

In the middle of enjoying a bagel and cream cheese, San-difer was suddenly convulsed with pain. Nausea flooded over her, and she abandoned her meal and dragged herself out to her car, where she waited for Jim to return.

After an eternity of agonizing pain, Jim showed up. Taking one look, he wanted to take her directly to the hospital, but Sandifer refused. It was proba-bly only a bout of intestinal flu, she reasoned. She was tough: She would get over it.

But her stomach pains didn't go away. Sandifer finally relented and sought medical help. To her consternation and growing alarm, the diagnosis eluded the doctor. Months of medical tests and consultations with specialists followed— along with the ever-present pain.

One of a long succession of doctors finally discovered that almost the entire length of Sandifer's sigmoid and ascend-ing colon—the long, bulbous gray organ that connects the stomach to the lower intes-tine—had for some unknown reason ceased functioning.

Nothing could be done to save it, and most of Sandifer's colon was surgically removed, leaving her with only 14 inches to perform the digestive work of a normal intestine. And now,

Healing Through the Power of Prayer

five years later, these last 14 inches were threatened by a tumor.

Sandifer did what many of us would do. She feared for her future and that of her family. And she prayed. But Sandifer chose not to bear her burden alone. She confided in a few trusted friends, including huge, gregarious John Vorlander, who had himself experienced the healing power of prayer in remarkable ways. Vorlander readily agreed to intercede in prayer for Sandifer's healing.

On Wednesday, Sandifer went to speak with her pastor, the Reverend David Harper. After listening sympathetically, he asked: "Joy, would you be satisfied with a colectomy?"

The question caught Sandifer off guard. Medical science offered only one option to someone in her condition—a colectomy. It is a surgical procedure that would reroute her remaining intestine. The idea horrified her.

"I don't think I could, David," answered Sandifer candidly. "How then would you like me to pray?" he inquired.

A picture came into Sandifer's mind of the fig tree in Jesus' parable. She opened her Bible and read the words of Jesus' disciple Peter: "Rabbi, look! The fig tree you cursed has withered!" (Mark 11:21).

Sandifer was no theologian and made no pretense of being able to fully interpret the meaning of the parable. But the imagery of the withered fig tree spoke to her heart. "I'd like you to pray that this tumor will wither and die like the fig tree in Jesus' parable."

Harper graciously agreed. Any reluctance he may have had about his parishioner's novel application of the biblical text soon vanished, for as they prayed together that day, he sensed a divine presence in their midst.

Alone in her home with time to meditate, Sandifer continued in prayer, ever aware of the deadly tumor. Did she have a right to trust that God would hear her petition? Sandifer believed that she did and based her conviction on biblical passages such as Philippians 4:6–7: "Do not worry about anything, but in everything by prayer and supplication, with thanksgiving let your requests be known to God. And the peace of God, which surpasses all understanding, will guard your hearts and your minds in Christ Jesus."

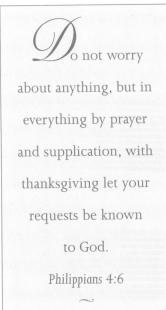

Do not worry about anything, but in everything by prayer and supplication, with thanksgiving let your requests be known to God.

Philippians 4:6

Verses like these were a wonderful comfort to Sandifer. And yet she knew she couldn't demand that God heal her. Her own previous surgery taught her that healing is not automatic. Many people who earnestly desire to be healed are not.

Joy Sandifer did not fall into the "either-or" trap—the attitude that either one trusts God for healing or one goes to a doctor. She realized that her Creator very often uses doctors as well as other components of modern medicine to heal people. She understood that perhaps this would be the way that her healing would come to her.

Healing Through the Power of Prayer

The next morning the phone rang. Sandifer glanced at the clock before she picked up the phone. It was ten o'clock. On the other end was an exuberant John Vorlander. "I believe the Lord has showed me that your tumor is gone! You have been healed!"

Sandifer was taken aback by her friend. She hardly dared to believe it could be true—and yet when Vorlander spoke, she felt a quiet confirmation in her spirit. She would not have long to wait: The next day would tell the story.

Sandifer had mixed feelings as she walked into the sterile examination room on Friday morning for her presurgical checkup. She believed that God had touched her, but could she have been mistaken? Would her fervent prayers and expectations for a miraculous healing be dashed?

After finishing his examination, her doctor looked at her with furrowed brow. "Well, this is very interesting," he said, "I can't seem to find anything." Sandifer's heart leapt within her. She blurted out, "I know why you can't. I've been healed!"

Her doctor brushed aside her explanation. "Tumors don't just disappear," he insisted. "It's probably hiding in a fold of the intestine." He instructed her to

> *S*he believed that God had touched her, but could she have been mistaken? Would her fervent prayers and expectations for a miraculous healing be dashed?

return at a later date for another examination, to which Sandifer agreed.

Three weeks later, her doctor and an associate performed another special test called a sigmoidoscopy to thoroughly examine her intestine. Once again they found nothing. Still not convinced, her doctor insisted she have another barium enema test—the same test that originally detected the tumor.

Sandifer agreed, but by this time had enough confidence in her healing that she put the test off until she returned from a long-planned trip to the Holy Land. The pilgrimage was a wonderful, life-changing experience for her. She gazed out over the same hills and fields of Galilee that Jesus had known and loved. It was there that the Bible says: "Many crowds followed him, and he cured all of them" (Matthew 12:15).

Biblical names came alive for her: the ancient fishing village of Capernaum where the Centurion's servant was healed; Jericho, where blind Bartimaeus received his sight; and Bethany, home of Lazarus, who was raised from the dead.

Sandifer believed in her heart that the Great Physician had also touched her. The final proof came after she returned home and had the barium enema performed. This time, in a complete reversal of the earlier test, the doctor's report stated: "There is no evidence of abnormal filling defect in the visualized portion of the rectum sigmoid or distal ileum. . . . No suspicious abnormality is suggested by the current examination."

Sandifer, who had by this time become familiar with the medical jargon associated with her condition, knew what this second report meant: Her intestine was completely free of all obstruction, and so it has remained to this day.

By all accounts, Joy Sandifer experienced a dramatic reversal of a life-threatening illness. Did God heal her? That is a controversial question, and even among Christians there is a wide variety of beliefs regarding the possibility of divine healing.

Morton Kelsey describes several different responses to the question "Does God heal?" The responses are worth examining. The first, which has been mentioned, is the denial of the possibility of miracles.

THE VIEW OF ORTHODOX MEDICINE

This perspective developed in our own century out of an unbounded confidence in the capabilities of modern science. As a result of advances in medicine between the years 1900 and 1956, the life expectancy of the average American jumped a full 20 years. By contrast, the death rate dropped to only one percent of the population per year. It was only a matter of time, it was assumed, before modern medicine would conquer all illness and all disease.

Or so it seemed. After all, the world was governed by predetermined laws, was it not? The human body was viewed as an intricate collection of physical processes that could be regulated by drugs, surgery, and other physical changes to the organism. To reverse disease, all that remained was to find the right chemical "keys" or surgical procedures. And in the twentieth century, medical science made gigantic strides

Healing Through the Power of Prayer

toward discovering the biological causes of disease.

Flushed with its successes, the medical profession downplayed the possibility of divine intervention in the material world. God—if there was a God—was not in the business of healing: That was the task of the medical community. The duty of the Church was to attend to matters of the soul. Religion had no business meddling in what was viewed as the rightful domain of modern science.

This supreme optimism in the power of medicine has begun to fade, tempered by the inability of medical researchers to find a cure for many dis-

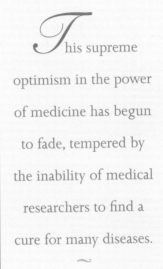

eases—perhaps most visibly with regard to the AIDS epidemic. Despite a budget of $1.6 billion, the National Cancer Institute has not only failed to find a cure for most cancers, but with few exceptions the overall mortality rate from the dreaded disease stubbornly refuses to diminish. Other diseases long thought to be virtually eradicated, such as tuberculosis, are once again on the increase. Another area of growing concern is antibiotics, once considered the "miracle drugs" that would eradicate biological

This supreme optimism in the power of medicine has begun to fade, tempered by the inability of medical researchers to find a cure for many diseases.

disease. We are now witnessing, however, an alarming increase of deadly strains of bacteria that are resistant to virtually all known antibiotics.

Despite the unrealized expectations of modern medicine, many even in the Church continue to view divine healing with suspicion, preferring to look to conventional medicine as their sole recourse for healing. Others take the opposite view: It is "unspiritual" to trust in doctors and medicine. We should, they say, go instead to the Great Physician for healing.

Yet there is a middle ground between these extremes—one that is grateful for the many benefits modern medicine has bestowed upon us and yet looks to the Ultimate Healer. According to this view, there are many occasions when God uses doctors and medicine as instruments of healing. And there are times when God may choose to heal us directly. The Book of Sirach offers wise, balanced advice regarding the medical profession:

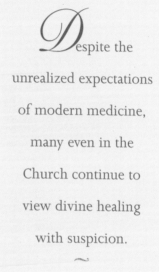

Despite the unrealized expectations of modern medicine, many even in the Church continue to view divine healing with suspicion.

"Honor physicians for their services,
for the Lord created them;
for their gift of healing comes
from the Most High,
and they are rewarded by the king.
The skill of physicians makes
them distinguished,

Healing Through the Power of Prayer

and in the presence of the
great they are admired.
The Lord created medicines out
of the earth,
and the sensible will not
despise them.
Was not water made sweet with
a tree
in order that its power might
be known?
And he gave skill to human
beings
that he might be glorified in
his marvelous works.
By them the physician heals
and takes away pain;
the pharmacist makes a
mixture from them.
God's works will never be
finished;
and from him health spreads
over all the earth.
My child, when you are ill, do
not delay,
but pray to the Lord, and he
will heal you.
Give up your faults and direct
your hands rightly,
and cleanse your heart from
all sin.
Offer a sweet-smelling sacrifice,
and a memorial portion of
choice flour,
and pour oil on your offer-
ing, as much as you can
afford.
Then give the physician his
place, for the Lord created
him;
do not let him leave you, for
you need him.
There may come a time when
recovery lies in the hands
of physicians,
for they too pray to the Lord
that he grant them success in
diagnosis
and in healing, for the sake
of preserving life"
(Sirach 38:1-14).

It is no exaggeration to state
that there has been no land or
people or culture where the
healing arts have not been
present. To be sure, many of the
potions and methods of dealing

Healing Through the Power of Prayer

with sickness would be regarded as primitive today. But it stands to reason that the healers also must have achieved some measure of success, otherwise they would not have survived as a profession. As the Book of Sirach states, numerous "medicinal herbs" are to be found in creation, which have been used by physicians since time immemorial. Thus the medical profession has been an important means—one could well say a divine provision—for bringing healing.

There is no necessary contradiction between relying directly upon God for healing and, at the same time, using doctors and medicine. Father Benedict Heron, in his book *Channels of Healing Prayer*, presents a balanced view of the use of medical care: "I am of the opinion that it is normally good to start by praying for healing. If we do this some-

times we shall find that the sickness disappears and that medicine and medical attention are not necessary. However, in certain circumstances it is of course very important not to delay seeking medical help. . . . But in these cases, pray on the way to the doctor or the hospital."[1]

Thus Father Heron combines prayer with seeking proper medical attention, being careful to add: "Obviously praying for healing must never stand in the way of people receiving the medical help they ought to have. Sometimes the most important thing we have to do is to tell someone to see a doctor."[2]

From time to time, news reports surface about those who have died or, even more tragic, allowed their children to perish as the result of refusing to obtain proper medical treatment on religious grounds.

There is no biblical warrant for denying medical care to ourselves or those we love because we believe it is the "spiritual" thing to do. As Father Heron advises, pray on the way to the doctor!

Since we do not know what channels our Creator may choose to bring healing, we should not cut ourselves off from what could potentially be God's choice for that particular circumstance. God may have prepared just the right doctor to cure us. Father Francis MacNutt, a Roman Catholic priest with a ministry of healing, relates one instance where God used a roundabout means of bringing healing. He prayed for a young man named Randy, who suffered from asthma. He was surprised to learn later that after he prayed, Randy had his most severe attack, so bad that his parents could not wait to see their regular doctor. They rushed him to a physician who lived down the street, who was able to correctly diagnose Randy's problem for the first time: "The prayer, then, had been answered in a way helpful to my humility: Randy got worse. But the prayer was answered: his getting

> *There is no biblical warrant for denying medical care to ourselves or those we love because we believe it is the "spiritual" thing to do. As Father Heron advises, pray on the way to the doctor!*

Healing Through the Power of Prayer

worse resulted in his getting another doctor, whom they wouldn't otherwise have consulted, who, in turn, discovered the correct diagnosis which eventually worked the cure. It was as if the effect of our prayer was to find the right doctor through whom God wanted to cure Randy."[3]

In Randy's case, God used medical science in a way that Father MacNutt did not foresee. Nevertheless, in the end his prayer for healing was answered. Like Father MacNutt, we should consider the healing arts to be a gift from God.

As the proper balance is sought regarding the relationship between conventional medicine and spiritual healing, it would seem that two extremes should be avoided. The first is ignoring or refusing to consider the spiritual dimension. After all, who can say with certainty that no reality exists outside of the three dimensions of our material universe? There exists for any open-minded searcher manifold testimony to the reality of divine healing. The second extreme is a false spirituality that seeks to "rely on God

Who can say with certainty that no reality exists outside of the three dimensions of our material universe? There exists for any open-minded searcher manifold testimony to the reality of divine healing.

Healing Through the Power of Prayer

alone." This attitude rejects the divine provision for our healing in the form of doctors and medicine. Harmful, even fatal, consequences can result in the event of either of these extremes. It is possible to miss out on a supernatural healing by not seeking it. Likewise, we can succumb to illness by refusing to consult doctors.

There is another response to the question of whether God heals: "It all depends." For people who subscribe to this belief, miracles can occur only if certain conditions are satisfied. Sickness is a necessary evil: It is God's punishment for sin.

SICKNESS AS DIVINE JUDGMENT

The notion that sickness is God's punishment for sin and disobedience has been with us for centuries. It was clearly expressed in the sixteenth-century *Book of Common Prayer*

commissioned by the Church of England. The *Book of Common Prayer* referred to sickness as "the chastisement of the Lord" that was meant to be endured by the faithful. The infirmed are exhorted to "patiently, and with thanksgiving, bear our heavenly Father's correction, whensoever by any manner of adversity it shall please his gracious good-ness to visit us."[4]

The priest administering the Office of the Visitation of the Sick was required to examine the patient to ensure that they held to the Apostle's Creed. If they did not, then medical assistance was withheld. But it soon proved too simplistic to attribute all sickness to theolog-ical or moral error. A contem-porary prayer book relates the unfortunate story of a man suffering from a heart attack who confessed his doubts as to the doctrine of the incarnation. This being the presumed cause

Healing Through the Power of Prayer

for his being stricken, the priest wasted no time in subjecting the poor man to several hours of instruction in the dogmas of the church. Despite the priest's efforts, however, shortly after he left the man expired.

The old form of the Visitation Office is rarely used anymore, but the attitude that sickness is God's punishment remains a prominent theme. Morton Kelsey writes that Agnes Sanford, one of the pioneer faith healers of the twentieth century, was willing to admit her own inability to heal: "If the person did not get well, she never blamed the sick person but concluded that she had not been an adequate channel of God's love. . . . She considered herself an inadequate but sometimes effective instrument of God's grace."[5]

Sanford's humility in being willing to accept part of the blame when those she prayed for were not healed is commendable. But we cannot let ourselves off the hook entirely. Most people would agree that our own foolish or sinful actions may account for at least some illness. After all, the detrimental health effects of smoking, obesity, and jaywalking are well established.

The Bible is replete with examples of disease and pestilence being the direct result of disobedience against God. In the Book of Exodus, for example, the Lord exhorts the

Most people would agree that our own foolish or sinful actions may account for at least some illness.

children of Israel to obey his commandments so that "I will not bring upon you any of the diseases I brought upon the Egyptians" (Exodus 15:26).

Other passages in the Bible, however, indicate that not all sickness and adversity is the result of sin. The Book of Job is the story of one man's catastrophic loss of his family and possessions, followed by severe physical affliction. The text, however, gives not the slightest indication that Job's suffering was the result of his sin. To the contrary, we read that "[Job] was blameless and upright, one who feared God and turned away from evil" (Job 1:1).

IS THE AGE OF MIRACLES PAST?

The idea that the Bible divides history into various eras is popular in some contemporary religious circles. This view teaches that God works in different ways at different times. For example, while God performed miracles in biblical times, they are no longer necessary in the present age. That is because they served as a "sign" to authenticate the teaching of the prophets and especially Jesus. But now we have the self-authenticating divine revelation in the form of the Bible to guide us.

The roots of this view may be traced to the Reformation. Martin Luther taught that the day of miracles was past, for "now that the apostles have preached the Word and have given their writings, and nothing more than what they have written remains to be revealed, no new and special revelation or miracle is necessary."[6] The Swiss Reformer John Calvin, Luther's contemporary, agreed.

The influence of the two pillars of the Reformation

Healing Through the Power of Prayer

regarding healing cannot be underestimated. They set the theological tone for centuries to come. With few exceptions, it remains the adopted view of much of Protestantism.

In his book *Faith Healing and the Christian Faith*, Dr. Wade Boggs argues that the purpose of miracles in the Book of Acts was to validate the preaching of the apostles. However, when the writings of the New Testament were completed, there no longer remained any purpose for miracles, which then ceased.[7]

ANOTHER LOOK

The evidence for the healing power of prayer today continues to accumulate.

And that is where the experi-  ence of people like Joy Sandifer enters the discussion. Stories like

hers can help formulate a view of divine healing that is both biblically informed and balanced. Her experience can be evaluated by asking a few questions (these questions will be addressed in more detail):

Was Sandifer actually healed? The medical records indicate that she was. According to the before and after barium enema tests and examinations by her doctors, a mass in her intestines clearly disappeared. Doctors use the term "spontaneous remission" when there is no known explanation for the disappearance of a known pathology. In Sandifer's case, however, there is an explanation that is at the very least highly coincidental: The tumor disappeared precisely when Joy and others were engaged in intensive prayer. Did a spontaneous remission just happen to occur when prayers for healing were being offered?

Healing Through the Power of Prayer

To adapt a saying: "If it walks like a miracle and talks like a miracle," one should be open-minded enough to at least admit the possibility that it is a miracle. In fact, the conclusion that Sandifer experienced something beyond the pale of conventional medicine—that she was healed—is eminently reasonable.

Does God always heal? Sandifer's own experience belies the idea that divine healing is guaranteed. Several years before the tumor was discovered, she had most of her intestine surgically removed. On that occasion, despite her prayers, God did not miraculously heal her. In

neither case was Sandifer aware of any sin on her part that might have caused the illness—yet on one occasion she was healed and the other she was restored to health through the aide of modern medicine. Beyond that, there is nothing more that can be said: The reason is hidden in the inscrutable divine will.

The belief that the only barrier to divine healing is sin or rebellion on the part of the sick individual can lead to unnecessary guilt and emotional suffering. Sin can be a

> *I*ndeed, the Bible indicates that sin does have physical, emotional, and spiritual consequences, and we do well to examine our consciences.

Healing Through the Power of Prayer

factor. Indeed, the Bible indicates that sin does have physical, emotional, and spiritual consequences, and we do well to examine our consciences. But if we are still not healed, there is no biblical warrant to blame ourselves.

If we can't blame ourselves for our illness, then who or what is responsible? It doesn't take a rocket scientist to figure out that the human population has some very serious problems. Violence, aggression, injustice, and a host of other evils are wreaking havoc all over. The reality of evil defies logical explanation. It's almost as if something behind the scenes is driving it—and according to the Bible—that is exactly what is happening. The Scriptures speak about powerful and destructive forces at work in the world.

These unseen powers have their origin in a primordial rebellion against God. Genesis tells the story of what theologians call the Fall.

The Apostle Paul wrote "sin came into the world through one man, and death came through sin" (Romans 5:12). Ultimately, all sickness and disease find their source in the curse of sin and death that came upon all of creation after Adam's

> *O*ur prayers are answered according to the divine will and purpose for our lives. While we are encouraged to bring our requests to our Creator, the answer must be left to him.

rebellion. We are all subject to the effects of that curse.

How important is faith in healing? James 1:6–8 is an oft-quoted passage to show the importance of faith: "But ask in faith, never doubting, for the one who doubts is like a wave of the sea, driven and tossed by the wind; for the doubter, being double-minded and unstable in every way, must not expect to receive anything from the Lord."

Faith is sometimes described as if it is something we "work up" inside ourselves. After we reach a "critical mass" of faith, then, we are assured, God will automatically hear and answer our prayers as we want him to. But woe to the poor individuals who somehow cannot seem to "work up enough faith." Doubt and confusion follow, along with self-condemnation and a subtle, unspoken critical attitude from their peers.

The insistence that God always heals drives some to extremes when they fail to experience healing. Some individuals plow full-steam ahead and claim healing regardless of their actual condition.

This ploy may work fine with many common illnesses that with time go away on their own. But with persistent and serious illnesses, the ruse cannot be maintained indefinitely, and sooner or later the sick individual is forced to face up to the facts. For those who sincerely believe all illness is the result of sin or a lack of faith, it can be personally devastating.

But James is not teaching that everything depends on how much faith we can "work up." Faith in this passage refers to faith in God, not in some supposed inner power to compel our Heavenly Father to do what we want.

Our prayers are answered according to the divine will and purpose for our lives. While we are encouraged to bring our requests to our Creator, the answer must be left to him. God cannot be manipulated into doing what we want. Sometimes the answer will be "yes"; on other occasions it will be "no."

Perhaps hardest of all is a third response: "wait." We would prefer to have an answer—*any* answer—rather than to exist in a state of uncertainty. We wonder if God has forgotten about our situation; we fear our case has gotten misplaced somehow and we are doomed to be perpetually on hold. But we must continue to hold on, with the expectation of good things ahead for us. In the words of the psalmist: "I believe that I shall see the goodness of the Lord in the land of the living. Wait for the Lord; be strong, and let your heart take courage; Wait for the Lord!" (Psalm 27:13–14).

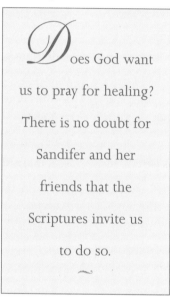

Does God want us to pray for healing? There is no doubt for Sandifer and her friends that the Scriptures invite us to do so.

Does God want us to pray for healing? There is no doubt for Sandifer and her friends that the Scriptures invite us to do so. The story of Hezekiah's healing, which will be discussed later, suggests that we need to take the initiative and make our requests known to our Maker. We read in the Book of James: "Are any among you sick? They should call for the elders of the church and have them pray over them, anointing them with oil in the name of the Lord. The prayer of faith will save the sick, and the Lord will raise them up" (James 5:14–15).

For Sandifer, the Bible tells the story of God's love for humanity: "The Lord gave us His Word not to read casually but to look at as a promise from someone who really loves us. God will answer us on all levels—not just the ethereal but the practical as well." And what is more practical and down-to-earth than healing—whether physically, emotionally, or spiritually? Sandifer's experience demonstrates how her healing was granted at her point of greatest need. Her remarkable story serves as inspiration for further exploration of the possibilities of healing through the power of prayer.

CHAPTER 3: God Cares for Our Body and Soul

Then Jesus went about all the cities
and villages, teaching in their
synagogues, and proclaiming the
good news of the kingdom,
and curing every disease and
every sickness.

Matthew 9:35

Hidden among the maze of dusty narrow streets in the Old City of Jerusalem lies a medieval cloister. Inside the high walls stands the magnificent church of St. Anne, the finest example of a Crusader church still standing in the Holy Land. Today, groups of

curious pilgrims make their way through the ancient streets to visit the unadorned basilica.

Next to the church lie the impressive ruins of the ancient Pool of Bethesda, spoken of in the gospels. Here Jesus healed a man who had been an invalid for 38 years: "When Jesus saw him lying there and knew that he had been there a long time, he said to him, 'Do you want to be made well?' The sick man answered him, 'Sir, I have no one to put me into the pool when the water is stirred; and while I am making my way, someone else steps down ahead of me.' Jesus said to him, 'Stand up! Take your mat and walk.' At once the man was made well, and he took up his mat and began to walk" (John 5:6–9).

In 1950, an archaeologist's spade uncovered a pagan sanctuary to the healing god Aesculapius, a minor but popular Greek god. It adjoins the Pool of Bethesda, and it dates to the time of Jesus.

In each of the more than 200 Aesculapian shrines scattered throughout ancient Greece and Rome, the sick and infirm would offer a sacrifice in a temple of Aesculapius, then they would immerse themselves in a ritual pool.

In all likelihood, the Aesculapian temple here also

accounts for the reason why Jesus encountered a great number of disabled people gathered there: The site had become a healing shrine.

A CLASH OF CULTURES

It is at the Pool of Bethesda that a radically new way of thinking about the human person is encountered. Consider how the people of Jesus' time looked at the world.

The Romans, who followed Greece on the stage of world history, were a practical people concerned more with empire-building than philosophical speculation. In Rome there was no equivalent of Mars Hill, the gathering place of philosophers in Athens. As a result, Rome added little to the philosophical worldview of their predeces-

Healing Through the Power of Prayer

sors. It adapted Greek mythology wholesale, giving Latinized names to the Greek gods: Zeus became Jupiter; Hermes was renamed Mercury; Artemis became Diana, etc.

Underlying the Greek mythology was a more formal philosophical worldview, which, for the Greeks, since the time of Plato had been built upon a dualism of mind and body. The individual consisted of a physical body as well as an eternal soul.

At first glance, this seems to have a lot in common with how Christians look at themselves and the world. After all, the Bible teaches that humans have a "soul" or spiritual nature as well as a body. But here is where the similarity ends.

The Greeks considered the material world to be of little value. It was an evil to be escaped. Salvation—if the Greeks considered the concept at all—had nothing to do with sin or one's relationship with God. The only thing people needed to be "saved" from was the body itself, which had become entrapped in the material world.

Sickness was considered a matter of fate: the affliction of those who incurred the displeasure of the capricious gods.

But this fatalistic attitude toward disease was cold comfort for those suffering

> *Salvation—if the Greeks considered the concept at all—had nothing to do with sin or one's relationship with God.*

Healing Through the Power of Prayer

from illness. What they needed was not impassive philosophy but concern for their very real needs. The cult of Aesculapius thrived precisely because it addressed the practical need for physical healing. This was the prevailing worldview into which Jesus came.

THE BIBLICAL WORLDVIEW

Jesus was raised with the religious and cultural perspective of the ancient Hebrews, which was vastly different from that of the Greeks. The Jewish people did not think of the human person as a soul and a body that, like oil and water, were completely separate and unmixed.

Accordingly, in Jewish law and tradition the body had real value and was accorded due respect. The Greeks and Romans didn't hesitate to destroy the mortal remains of the individual by cremation. The Hebrews, on the other hand, preserved the body of the individual through burial.

The fact that Jesus came to us in human form further establishes the importance of the body. The implications are staggering because, for example, in the East the body was nothing more than the temporary abode of a transient soul, which is meant to be periodically disposed of like a snake sheds its skin.

This revolutionary idea of the significance of the body as well as the soul is found to be affirmed throughout the New Testament: "Do you not know that you are God's temple and that God's Spirit dwells in you? If anyone destroys God's temple, God will destroy that person. For God's temple is holy, and you are that temple" (1 Corinthians 3:16–17).

The value placed upon the body goes to the heart of Chris-

Healing Through the Power of Prayer

tianity. "Every spirit that con-
fesses that Jesus Christ has
come in the flesh is of God,
and every spirit that does not
confess Jesus is not from God"
(1 John 4:2–3).

The raising of
Jesus from the
dead demon-
strates that our
bodies are not
disposable. The
New Testament
teaches there will
be a resurrection
of the dead at the
end of the age:
"If the Spirit of
him who raised
Jesus from the
dead dwells in
you, he who
raised Christ from the dead will
give life to your mortal bodies
also through his Spirit, that
dwells in you" (Romans 8:11).

Our bodies, therefore, are
not superfluous but should be
considered as a sacred trust,
worthy of all efforts to main-
tain and heal them. Through
the centuries, Christians have
acknowledged this hope for
restoration of the body as well
as the soul in
their prayers. In
the Holy Com-
munion service
of the Anglican
church, the
words "[May]
the body of our
Lord, Jesus
Christ . . . pre-
serve thy body
and soul unto
everlasting life"
are spoken when
the bread and
wine are admin-
istered to the congregation.

We are also assured in the
writings of St. Paul that "The
last enemy to be destroyed is
death" (1 Corinthians 15:26).
Therefore, the effects of sick-

> *O*ur bodies,
> therefore, are not
> superfluous but should
> be considered as a
> sacred trust, worthy of
> all efforts to maintain
> and heal them.

Healing Through the Power of Prayer

ness and disease that eventually lead to death are also to be considered an "enemy" that is ultimately contrary to the will of God. He is concerned with the total person, the body as well as the soul.

In the ancient world, the cult of Aesculapius drew its popularity by standing in opposition to the Greco-Roman view of the body.

But at the Pool of Bethesda, Aesculapius met his match in the Great Physician who alone was able to heal the paralytic. And if he can heal the paralytic, he can heal us.

CHAPTER 4: Jesus' Healing Ministry

> He welcomed them, and spoke to
> them about the kingdom of God,
> and healed those who needed
> to be cured.
>
> Luke 9:11

Nestled along the northern shores of the Sea of Galilee at the foot of the valley of Korazin lies the remains of an ancient fishing hamlet with the name of Kefar Nahum ("village of Nahum"). Known as Capernaum by readers of the New Testament, the seemingly  insignificant village was overshadowed by larger cities on the lake, such as Magdala and Tiberius to the south.

It is here where Jesus went to live after his decisive rejection at Nazareth. We read in the Gospel of Luke that the enraged inhabitants of the city tried to throw him off a cliff after he applied the prophecy of Isaiah to himself: "The Spirit of the Lord is upon me, because he has anointed me to bring good news to the poor. He has sent me to proclaim release to the captives and recovery of sight to the blind, to let the oppressed go free, to proclaim the year of the Lord's favor" (Luke 4:18–19).

What did Jesus really mean here? Some see Jesus' use of this passage, which speaks of "release to the captives" and freeing the oppressed, as a manifesto for insurrection against the heavy-handed Roman occupation of Palestine. Indeed, many in Jesus' day looked for a messiah figure who would instigate such a revolt. History records several messiah figures, including Judas Maccabee and Bar Kochba, who led the Jewish people in bloody and unsuccessful uprisings.

But this view is untenable in the light of Jesus' steadfast refusal to allow himself to be cast as a political messiah. When questioned by Pontius Pilate as to whether he consid-

ered himself to be the king of the Jews, he replied: "My kingdom is not from this world. If my kingdom were from this world, my followers would be fighting to keep me from being handed over to the Jews. But as it is, my kingdom is not from here" (John 18:36).

If by quoting Isaiah Jesus was not advocating revolution, then what was he talking about? We find the key in another response of Jesus when questioned about the kingdom of God: "The kingdom of God is not coming with things that can be observed; nor will they say, 'Look, here it is!' or 'There it is!' For, in fact, the kingdom of God is among you" (Luke 17:20–21).

The kingdom of God is among you. The transformation Jesus was talking about when he quoted

Healing Through the Power of Prayer

Isaiah was not of a political system but of the individual. We can safely assume that "the recovery of sight to the blind" is a reference to physical healing, as we have numerous recorded instances of Jesus doing exactly that.

On the other hand, the terms "release to the captives" and "let the oppressed go free" raise yet another point of interest since we know Jesus did not go around freeing prisoners. Those phrases must be taken to refer to freedom from psychological and spiritual bondage.

Jesus' application of the Isaiah passage to himself affirms that he came to minister to the whole person, both body and soul. Inexplicably, and this is part of what theologians call "the Mystery of Evil," many of his countrymen did not accept Jesus. He experienced a profound rejection at Nazareth because many were not prepared to accept the transformation he came to offer. Why any of us sometimes refuse what would be good and beneficial for us can truly be called a mystery.

Pilgrims to the Holy Land can visit the northern end of the Sea of Galilee, where, again, Jesus' ministry did not have the intended effect: "Then he began to reproach the cities in which most of his deeds of

> *Jesus' application of the Isaiah passage to himself affirms that he came to minister to the whole person, both body and soul.*

Healing Through the Power of Prayer

power had been done, because they did not repent. 'Woe to you, Chorazin! Woe to you Bethsaida! For if the deeds of power done in you had been done in Tyre and Sidon, they would have repented long ago in sackcloth and ashes . . . . And you, Capernaum, will you be exalted to heaven? No, you will be brought down to Hades. For if the deeds of power done in you had been done in Sodom, it would have remained until this day. But I tell you that on the day of judgment it will be more tolerable for the land of Sodom than for you'" (Matthew 11:21,23–24).

Jesus desired that his miracles would have a life-transforming effect on those who experienced them. Sadly, all too often this was not the case. Given the large number of miracles that the gospels say he performed, and given the rather small geographic area of Galilee, there could not have been many extended families that were not touched by Jesus' ministry. Given the continuing widespread skepticism and opposition to his ministry, we can only conclude that some who experienced healing in their own family must have rejected him. As inconceivable as it may seem, even those who saw family members wonderfully healed did not have thankful hearts.

Jesus uses another incident to highlight the lack of thankfulness on the part of those who received healing: "On the way to Jerusalem Jesus was going through the region between Samaria and Galilee. As he entered a village, ten lepers approached him. Keeping their distance, they called out, saying, 'Jesus, Master, have mercy on us!' When he saw them, he said to them, 'Go and show yourselves to the priests.'

Healing Through the Power of Prayer

And as they went, they were made clean. Then one of them, when he saw that he was healed, turned back, praising God with a loud voice. He prostrated himself at Jesus' feet and thanked him. And he was a Samaritan. Then Jesus asked, 'Were not ten made clean? But the other nine, where are they? Was none of them found to return and give praise to God except for this foreigner?' Then he said to him, 'Get up and go on your way; your faith has made you well'" (Luke 17:11–19).

And he was a Samaritan. The Samaritans were Jews who centuries before had intermarried with Gentiles and thus were not of pure Jewish descent. The Jews looked at the Samaritans with contempt and would not so much as traverse their territory. The ancient Jewish route from their territory in Galilee to Jerusalem skirted Samaritan territory, and it is here as he was "going through the region between Samaria and Galilee" that Jesus encountered the lepers.

It was the Samaritan who returned to Jesus and gave praise to God. A man who was a double pariah, both from his leprosy and his race, was the one who received Jesus' praise and blessing: "Get up and go on your way; your faith has made you well."

There is a lesson here for us: Regardless of how unwanted and insignificant we may feel, or how others may reject us, there is One who cares and accepts us. Jesus spent little of his time in the citadels of power or networking with those who could perhaps promote his ministry with the chief priests in Jerusalem. Though he turned no one away, more often than not he was found in the villages and countryside among the common everyday people.

Jesus' love for the poor and the ordinary should be an inspiration to us all. We do not have to have wealth or success to have value in God's eyes.

FOR EACH A BALM

Reading through the gospels, on almost every page we see Jesus performing miracles. It is impossible to escape the importance of healing to his ministry. There are 41 distinct references to people being healed of various diseases in the gospels. A full one-third of the Gospel of Luke is devoted to Jesus' healings.

Jesus' love for the poor and the ordinary should be an inspiration to us all. We do not have to have wealth or success to have value in God's eyes.

It is interesting to note that Luke was a physician and would naturally have taken a special interest in physical healings. The fact that he was a doctor adds to the credibility of his account, for his medical experience would have aided him in weeding out accounts that were not genuine. Indeed, at the beginning of his gospel we read: "Since many have undertaken to set down an orderly account of the events that have been fulfilled among us, just as they were handed on to us by those who from the beginning were eyewitness and servants of the word, I too decided, after investigating everything carefully from the very first, to write an orderly account for you, Theophilus, so that you may know the truth concerning the things about which you have been interested" (Luke 1:1–4).

Scholars have little idea of who Theophilus was. Some have suggested he was a government official who converted to the new Christian faith. We also do not know exactly when Luke's gospel was written, but we do know that he was a traveling companion of the Apostle Paul. That would put him in the same generation as those who witnessed the miracles of Jesus. Thus it is entirely reasonable to accept his claim to have "carefully investigated" the events of Jesus' life.

But it is in the Gospel of Mark that we see the greatest emphasis upon miracles of healing. In the brief 15 chapters of this gospel, we encounter no fewer than 24 instances where Jesus confronted the physical and mental maladies of those who came to him.

It is sometimes asked whether there is a certain method or formula that must be followed in order for healing to occur. We certainly have no indication of this by examining Jesus' healing ministry. The recorded healings occur under a remarkable variety of circumstances: No "standard operating procedure" is evident. Jesus adapts his method of healing to the needs of each situation, addressing the specific needs of those who come to him.

His most common method of healing seems to have been a combination of speaking words of healing and touching the individual. Sometimes Jesus lays hands upon the sick person; on other occasions he merely touches the eyes of a blind man or the tongue of a deaf-mute. But sometimes he does not touch the person at all, as in the exorcism of the Syrophoenician woman's daughter (Mark 7:25–30). And on at least one occasion, that of the woman who was hemorrhaging, the woman is healed simply by touching Jesus' cloak (Mark 5:27–34).

In three instances, Jesus employs what is to our twentieth-century mentality a peculiar method of bringing healing. He uses his saliva, either alone or mixed with dirt to make a paste. Curiously, in those days, both saliva and certain kinds of earth were thought to have medicinal properties. This raises an intriguing question: Why was Jesus using what those of his day considered to be a form of "medicine?" Could there also be occasions in our day when we assume that a particular medicine is healing us but in reality a far greater power is responsible?

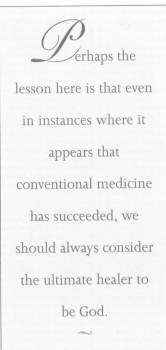

Perhaps the lesson here is that even in instances where it appears that conventional medicine has succeeded, we should always consider the ultimate healer to be God.

Perhaps the lesson we learn is that even in instances where it appears that conventional medicine has succeeded, we should always consider the ultimate healer to be God.

Morton Kelsey suggests that Jesus' use of saliva and mud

was "not so much as a direct healing agent as a carrier of his personality and power."[1] It resembles other healing miracles such as Elisha telling the Syrian Naaman to bathe in the River Jordan (2 Kings 5:10), or King Hezekiah being told by Isaiah to apply a poultice of figs to his diseased skin (2 Kings 20:7). In each of these instances, few modern doctors would consider the action in itself to have much healing value. In each case, however,

> *The Book of Hebrews encourages us to "approach with a true heart in full assurance of faith" so that our prayers will be heard.*
>
> *Hebrews 10:22*

the medium served to demonstrate the power of the healer.

Olive oil was another common healing agent in the time of Jesus, and while we have no specific references to oil, it is likely that he used oil in healing. We read that when he sent out his disciples they "cast out many demons, and anointed with oil many who were sick and cured them" (Mark 6:13). Anointing with oil for healing was practiced by the early churches. As we have already seen in the passage in James, the sick person was encouraged to "call for the elders of the church and have them pray over them, anointing them with oil in the name of the Lord. The prayer of faith will save the sick, and the Lord will raise them up" (James 5:14–15).

The confident tone of this passage is striking. Some take this verse as absolute proof that God will always heal if we have enough faith. But experience teaches us that not all who pray are healed, even those who are anointed with oil. So what could be the meaning of this verse?

As will be suggested more fully later, the faith that is spoken of here is faith in God. It is not some power that we "work up" inside ourselves that will compel the Divine to do what we want. It may be that the "prayer of faith" refers to an inner, divine confirmation that in this instance God intends to heal. It has nothing to do with how much faith we have "built up" inside. God cannot be manipulated—even by well-intentioned prayers.

Those with the gift of healing are aware of occasions when their prayers for healing seem to "ring true"; they seem to have more confidence that in that particular case God intends to answer them. And there are other occasions when their prayers do not seem to penetrate the ceiling.

Is this because the healer is having an off day? More likely, there are times when our prayers coincide with the divine purpose for our lives and the lives of others, just as there are times when God has something else—and ultimately better—in mind.

We are once again thrown back upon the truth that the divine purposes are beyond our comprehension. But all this is not to suggest that we should not present our petitions to our

Healing Through the Power of Prayer

Heavenly Father with all earnestness. The Book of Hebrews encourages us to "approach with a true heart in full assurance of faith" so that our prayers will be heard (Hebrews 10:22).

HEALING FOR BODY, SOUL, AND SPIRIT

The Gospel of Mark records numerous healings in private homes at Capernaum. These private homes are called "insuli" by archaeologists. Visitors to the site can view these insuli, which are actually large enclosed dwellings built to accommodate extended families of up to 100 people. It was in one of these insuli that Jesus healed Simon Peter's mother-in-law of a fever.

Word spread and multitudes of people converged on the site. We read that "the whole city was gathered around the door. And he cured many who were sick with various diseases" (Mark 1:33–34).

Here, as throughout the gospels, we see Jesus ministering to everyone who came to him: We do not

> *H*ere, as throughout the gospels, we see Jesus ministering to everyone who came to him: We do not have even a single instance of him refusing to heal even though he must often have been exhausted from the constant demands of his followers.

have even a single instance of him refusing to heal even though he must often have been exhausted from the constant demands of his followers. We do, however, read that on occasions he felt the need to get away from people: "he got up and went out to a deserted place, and there he prayed" (Mark 1:35). Through the centuries, Christians have followed his example by participating in retreats for spiritual renewal.

A few days after healing the sick at Capernaum, Jesus returned home from a trip through Galilee only to be besieged once again by those desiring to be healed. Mark records an ingenious method that the friends of a paralytic employed to bring the infirmed man to Jesus' attention: "So many gathered around that there was no longer room for them, not even in front of the door; and he was speaking the word to them. Then some people came, bringing to him a paralyzed man, carried by four of them. And when they could not bring him to Jesus because of the crowd, they removed the roof above him; and, after having dug through it, they let down the mat on which the paralytic lay. When Jesus saw their faith, he said to the paralytic, 'Son, your sins are forgiven'" (Mark 2:2–5).

Note that on this occasion, Jesus heals the paralytic not on the basis of his own faith alone but upon seeing the faith of his companions. This suggests that we should not attempt to "go it alone" in our quest for healing. If we become sick, do we let others know so they can pray for us? The faith and prayers of those around us can play a decisive role in our restoration.

Jesus' fame as a healer spread so far and wide that, when traveling throughout Galilee, he "could no longer go into a town openly, but stayed out in the country; and people came to him from every quarter" (Mark 1:45).

Why did people flock to Jesus? There were numerous rabbis (religious teachers) who were seeking disciples. As revolutionary as Jesus' teaching was, it was in many cases not his message that drew them. They came for the healings: either to be healed themselves or to see others being healed. There must have been times when a carnival atmosphere prevailed as the sick, the curious, and the gawkers jostled one another to get as close to Jesus as possible.

Whatever the motive, those who followed him knew that Jesus was not just another religious teacher or "rabbi" preaching to them. He cared about their body—their physical needs. Not only were they healed, but on occasion they were even miraculously fed—as the feeding of the 5,000 testifies (Mark 6:30–44).

This concern for both body and soul was the hallmark of Jesus' followers from the very earliest days. As he trained his disciples to continue his work, healing was to be the heart of their mission.

This concern for both body and soul was the hallmark of Jesus' followers from the very earliest days of his ministry. As he trained his disciples to continue his work, healing was to be the heart of their mission, as it was his. He sent them out, commanding them to "cure the sick, raise the dead, cleanse the lepers, cast out demons. . . ." (Matthew 10:8).

As the Church moved beyond the age of the New Testament, the writings of the early Christians abounded with reports of healings. Miracles were not the domain of controversial fringe groups: They were an expected and vital aspect of the ministry of the whole Church.

But gradually the fire died. Over a period of several centuries, the attitude of the Christian community toward healing gradually changed.

CHAPTER 5:
Healing Through
the Ages

Then Jesus summoned his twelve
disciples and gave them authority
over unclean spirits, to cast them
out, and to cure every disease and
every sickness.

Matthew 10:1

Physical and emotional healing have always been central to the stories passed down through centuries of believers. Just as God performed miracles among his people through Moses and Aaron, and through Jesus and his disiciples,  he was at work after the last biblical pages were written. His miracles have been recorded by the faithful so that we (and indeed those who come after us) can read about God's power and know that it is always available. These stories are meant to encourage us and restore our faith.

Consider first Augustine of Hippo, who lived between A.D. 354 and 430. In his greatest work, *The City of God*, he makes a surprising admission regarding miracles in his own diocese: "I realized how many miracles were occurring in our own day and which were so like the miracles of old and also how wrong it would be to allow the memory of these marvels of divine power to perish from among our people. It is only two years ago that the keeping of records was begun here in Hippo, and already, at this writing, we have nearly seventy attested miracles."[1]

The story of these miracles has been pieced together from Latin sources by Morton Kelsey. It begins with the discovery in 415 of the mortal remains of St. Stephen, the first Christian martyr. In ancient times, as well as today in some Catholic churches, the venerated remains, or relics, of saints were placed in a newly consecrated church.

A shrine containing the relics of St. Stephen was placed in

Augustine's church at Hippo. Nothing out of the ordinary seems to have occurred until two weeks before Easter in the year 424, when two young people, a brother and sister, arrived in Hippo. They both suffered from convulsive seizures.

On Easter morning, as the church service was about to begin, the young man was found praying at the shrine of St. Stephen. Suddenly, he collapsed, and the congregation feared that he had expired. But he soon stood up, apparently cured of the seizures.

During a service several days later, Augustine asked the brother and sister to stand up in front of the church. The young man was quiet, but unfortunately his sister still trembled uncontrollably.

They sat down, and Augustine began his sermon but was interrupted by a piercing scream. The young woman had made her way to the shrine to pray and had the same experience as her brother. After screaming, she, too, fell to the ground, only to rise up completely healed. As the young woman stood before them the second time, Augustine records the joyous reaction of the congregation: "Praise to God was shouted so loud that my ears could scarcely stand the din."[2]

Augustine also wrote about a blind man in Milan who "was given back his sight; and so many other things of this kind have happened, even in this present time, that it is not possible for us either to know of all of them...."[3]

One other interesting detail regarding the healing of the blind man at Milan emerges from other accounts. It seems that the man, named Severus, was healed by touching his handkerchief to the funeral bier of St. Stephen.

Does God really use handkerchiefs to heal? The answer is, surprisingly, "Yes!" There is in fact a biblical reference to this phenomenon: "God did extraordinary miracles through Paul, so that the handkerchiefs or aprons that had touched his skin were brought to the sick, their diseases left them, and the evil spirits came out of them" (Acts 19:11–12).

> Since the earliest days, great people of faith have constituted an unbroken witness to the miraculous.

Some traditions would prefer to dismiss this aspect of Paul's ministry as well as the healing powers of the bones of saints. But there is a similar incident involving the healing power of bones recorded in the Old Testament: "Now bands of Moabites used to invade the land in the spring of the year. As a man was being buried, a marauding band was seen and the man was thrown into the grave of Elisha; as soon as the man touched the bones of Elisha, he came to life and stood on his feet" (2 Kings 13:20–21).

It does appear that on at least one occasion the bones of a man of God had miraculous properties. And if we cannot dismiss this Old Testament account, isn't it possible that God could work the same way on other occasions? Sometimes God chooses to use unusual means to bring about healing.

Just as writer Morton Kelsey documented reports of the miraculous powers of relics dating from the time of Augustine, so have others.[4] In fact, since the earliest days, great people of faith have constituted an unbroken witness to the miraculous.

Far from being uneducated and gullible, Justin Martyr was a deeply religious man who taught philosophy in Rome, the most cosmopolitan city of his day. Martyr attested to a wide variety of healings, including the raising of the dead. In his *Apology*, addressed to the emperor in Rome, he wrote of the power that Christians exercised over disease, which, in the emperor's ignorance, he attributed to demonic powers: "For numberless demoniacs throughout the whole world, and in your city, many of our Christian men exorcizing them in the Name of Jesus Christ . . . have

Healing Through the Power of Prayer

healed and do heal, rendering helpless and driving the possessing devils out of the men, though they could not be cured by all the other exorcists, and those who used incantations and drugs."[5]

The list of those who accepted the reality of divine healing is long. Morton Kelsey tells us: "They wrote about all kinds of experiences that showed how God had acted and continued to act in Christian lives, including much that was lively and down to earth. Healing of physical illness and the ability to relieve 'demon possession' are spoken of again and again in the more important works and referred to in some way by all these writers."[6]

THE HEALING TOUCH

A famous incident early in the life of Martin of Tours, a contemporary of Augustine, illustrates his remarkable character. Martin had been enlisted by his father into the Roman army at the age of 15, a not uncommon experience for a young man in those days. One wintry evening, three years later, Martin saw a freezing beggar lying exposed to the harsh elements.

Contemplating the poor man, Martin knew he had a decision to make, and he did not hesitate. Taking off his heavy military tunic, Martin cut it in two and shared it with the beggar.

That same night, Martin had a vision of Christ wearing the cloak he had given away. The incident affected him so profoundly that upon his discharge from the army, he entered a monastery. Eventually, against his wishes, he was made bishop of Tours by popular acclaim.

Few people know that Martin possessed a remarkable gift of

healing. He even raised to life a young man who had died after a brief illness: "Then laying hold, as it were, of the Holy Spirit, with the whole powers of his mind, he orders the others to quit the cell in which the body was lying; and bolting the door, he stretched himself at full length on the dead limbs of the departed brother. Having given himself for some time to earnest prayer, and perceiving by means of the Spirit of God that power was present, he then rose up a little, and gazing on the countenance of the deceased, he waited without misgiving for the result of his prayer and of the mercy of the Lord. And scarcely had the space of two hours elapsed, when he saw the dead man begin to move a little in all his members, and to tremble with his eyes opened. . . ."[7]

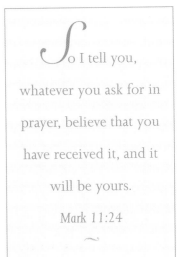

So I tell you, whatever you ask for in prayer, believe that you have received it, and it will be yours.

Mark 11:24

It is easy to dismiss this account as too fantastic to be believed. After all, would God really lead someone to use such unorthodox methods for healing? For the answer we need only to look at the remarkably similar parallel of Elisha's raising of the Shunammite woman's son from the dead: "When Elisha came into the house, he saw the child lying dead on his bed. So he went in and closed the door on the two of them, and prayed to the Lord. Then he got up on the bed and lay upon

Healing Through the Power of Prayer

the child, putting his mouth upon his mouth, his eyes upon his eyes, and his hands upon his hands; and while he lay bent over him, the flesh of the child became warm. He got down, walked once to and fro in the room, then got up again and bent over him; the child sneezed seven times, and the child opened his eyes" (2 Kings 4:32–35).

The question must be considered: If unusual healing miracles were performed in biblical times, why should similar miracles not have taken place in the centuries just after the death of Christ? And, taking the question a step further, if they were truly genuine then—and most Christians would agree that

they were— then wouldn't they also be genuine miracles now?

ARE WE HEALED OF SIN OR SICKNESS?

The thinking in the Church began to change regarding the gift of healing. It was not because the genuineness of miracles that had been performed for centuries was being questioned. It was rather that a different view of sickness arose. In the reign of Gregory the Great, bishop of Rome between 590 and 604, a new attitude began to take root.

Gregory lived during a time of social crisis: The once-invincible Roman Empire was being shaken to its very foundation. The unthinkable had already occurred with the sacking of Rome by barbarians from the northern frontiers. On every front, it seemed the empire was under siege.

Many people felt that God was punishing the Christianized Roman Empire for moral and doctrinal laziness. Illness came to be viewed as yet another means of divine punishment. As Gregory writes: "The sick are to be admonished that they feel themselves to be sons of God in that the scourge of discipline chastises them."[8]

His statement does reflect the teaching of the Book of Hebrews regarding chastisement: "My child, do not regard lightly the discipline of the Lord, or lose heart when you are punished by him; for the Lord disciplines those whom he loves, and chastises every child whom he accepts" (Hebrews 12:5–6).

During the Middle Ages, the view of sickness as

divine punishment predominated Western Christianity. In 1215, the Fourth Lateran Council formally adopted the position that "bodily infirmity is sometimes caused by sin." The council decreed that before physicians treat the sick, they should first summon a priest, on the grounds that "the cause [of illness] being removed the effect will pass away."[9]

My child, do not regard lightly the discipline of the Lord, or lose heart when you are punished by him; for the Lord disciplines those whom he loves, and chastises every child whom he accepts.

Hebrews 12:5–6

Healing Through the Power of Prayer

If they were right and sickness was indeed the sign of divine judgment, then earth was soon to become a nightmarish hell for many of its inhabitants. In October 1347, ships from Genoa put into port at the harbor of Messina, Sicily. Their arrival would soon change the face of the medieval world, for these ships brought with them an unseen enemy. It would claim more victims than had died in all the wars on the continent combined, up until that day.

For two years, the Black Death ravaged Europe, killing an estimated 20 million people. Physicians were powerless to cure the sick, many of whom perished with astonishing rapidity: Within 48 hours of exhibiting initial symptoms, most people suffered an agonizing death. It is estimated that up to a third of the world's population eventually succumbed to what modern medical science has identified as the bubonic and pneumonic plagues.

As the scale of the calamity exceeded the Church's worst nightmare, the Church remained steadfast in its conviction that the plague was sent by God. The Pope acknowledged it in a Bull of September 1348, speaking of the "pestilence with which God is afflicting the Christian people." The Emperor considered it "a

> *A*ccording to the Bible, sin can indeed be a cause of illness, but it is only one of several possible contributing factors.

Healing Through the Power of Prayer

malady of such horrors, stenches and agonies, and especially one bringing the dismal despair that settled on its victims before they died, was not a plague 'natural' to mankind but a 'chastisement from Heaven.'"[10]

This attitude still persists today. According to the Bible, sin can indeed be a cause of illness, but it is only one of several possible contributing factors. When focused upon as the exclusive cause of illness, it can lead to an overwhelming sense of emotional distress and hopelessness. Any lack of balance and perspective with regard to the reasons we suffer physically or emotionally could lead some of us to the brink of despair. That is not now, nor was it ever, part of God's plan for us.

Accounts of healings that occurred over many millenia should serve only as encouragement. God would not dangle these stories before us in order for us to long for something we could never have.

CHAPTER 6: There's No Turning Back!

"I will repay you for the years that the swarming locust has eaten."

Joel 2:25

Harold Hughes pulled into his driveway, shut off the engine, and sat in the darkness. The house, dark and empty, reminded him of the despair in his soul. Finally, he made his way to the front door. When she knew he would be coming home drunk, his wife, Eva, left with their little daughters to her mother's house until he could sober up.

As he stumbled inside, Harold remembered once again through his alcoholic daze why this evening was so important to Eva. Guilt washed over him as he thought of the dinner invitation missed. Because of his heavy drinking, they no longer had much of a social life, and she had looked forward so much to the chance to get out once again.

Eva had been cautiously optimistic that the invitation could signal the beginning of the long road back for them as a family. After all, Harold had sworn off drinking. He hadn't had one for the past two weeks.

Harold's modest success had generated overconfidence in his ability to withstand temptation. Thus, after a hard day at the office, some colleagues invited him out for a drink, and he agreed. "What harm could it do to sit at the bar for a moment?" he reasoned.

In the pleasant, familiar surroundings of the bar he relaxed. He decided there was no use trying to be a saint about it. He agreed to have just one drink and promised himself to say goodbye to his friends after that.

The bourbon tasted good. Harold realized how much he'd missed nursing a drink and the warm glow that followed. One drink led to another, and before he knew it, he heard someone announcing the time: It was 11 o'clock. Harold stumbled out into the parking lot and drove home.

Inside the empty house, Harold crumpled onto the

living room sofa. He felt sick. Despair washed over him as he thought of all the hard work that Eva had put into sewing the new dress that she had planned to wear that evening.

Once again he'd failed her—desperately. It was the same old story. Hughes cursed his addiction to alcohol. How many times had he sworn off drinking, promising his wife, Eva, that he would never touch another drop? Hughes slouched on the couch, bemoaning his failure.

The shame burned into him as he faced up to the reality of Harold Hughes: a father in his early thirties dogged by a crippling addiction throughout his adult life. Behind his back, people joked about his drinking problem. The sparkle had gone out of Eva's eyes as she

Healing Through the Power of Prayer

tired of seeing her surly husband dragging himself home reeking of alcohol and looking for a fight.

Harold was no stranger to despair, but something this evening pushed him over the edge. Inner voices tormented him: His life was worse than meaningless—he was a blight on everyone he knew.

Wandering into their bedroom, he thought once again of the lovely dress that Eva had sewn, her hopes for the evening shattered. Disgust for what he had become tore at him. He was no good: He would never change. Sprawled on the bed, a terrible thought came to him: If he couldn't do anything right, why not just end it all?

A cold logic seemed to take control of his actions; he ignored the protestations that screamed from another part of him. He was an evil man who only brought evil to those he loved. They would be better off without him, he believed. He rose and went to his closet. Inside were his rifle and shotgun.

"Better use the shotgun—it is the most certain," said the inner voices. With a strange detachment, as though he were observing himself from some outside vantage point, Harold reached for his single-barrel, 12-gauge Remington pump gun. Pumping a shell into the chamber, he walked into the bathroom and climbed into the tub. Tears streamed down his face; he hated what he was about to do almost as much as he hated himself. "There's no turning back now," hissed the inner demons.

Lying there, Harold positioned the Remington with the muzzle pointing in his mouth. His head was swimming as he reached for the trigger.

"Pull it!" He hesitated, filled with an inconsolable remorse. There didn't seem to be any other choice but to end it all.

Harold gazed down at the cold steel barrel. His family would get over it, he reasoned. With him gone, they would finally have an opportunity to rebuild their lives. By remaining, he would only hurt them more.

The inner voices egged him on, but just then an inexplicable thought came through. His upbringing had taught him that suicide was a sin: If there was a God, then he had better explain why he was about to end his own life in hopes that he would be forgiven. But he couldn't do that with a gun in his mouth. Harold climbed out of the tub and knelt on the tile floor, resting his head on the rim of the tub.

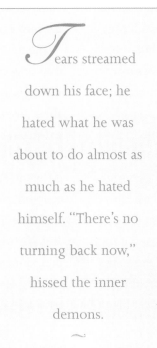

Tears streamed down his face; he hated what he was about to do almost as much as he hated himself. "There's no turning back now," hissed the inner demons.

He started to pray, and as he did the dam broke. He choked and started to cry, then began sobbing uncontrollably. "Oh, God," he groaned, "I'm a failure, a drunk, a liar, and a cheat. I'm lost, and hopeless, and want to die. Forgive me for doing this . . ." Harold collapsed on the floor, weeping and crying out to God until his voice gave out. He had no idea how much time passed as he

Healing Through the Power of Prayer

lay there quiet and still. A peace like he had never known settled over him, melting away the self-loathing and guilt.

Harold knew that he was experiencing the healing touch of God—forgiving him, changing him, and giving him another chance. He rose to a kneeling position and prayed, weeping, "Whatever you ask me to do, Father, I will do it."[1]

He got up and saw the weapon in the tub, shuddering to think that he had been an instant away from death. He unloaded it and returned it to the closet. As he did, the voices taunted, "Coward! Afraid to pull the trigger!" But another, more powerful voice assured him: "Stay with God, follow Him, *believe*."

Kneeling once again at his bed, Harold prayed: "Father, I don't understand this or know why I deserve it. For You know how weak I am. But I put myself back in your hands. Please give my family back to me . . . and give me the strength never to run again. Father, I put myself in your hands."[2] Harold crawled into bed and promptly fell into a deep, restful sleep.

The next morning, he realized how close he had come to killing himself. The old fears about his drinking problem began to assert themselves. But he knew this time things were different. He had had an encounter with the Living God.

Eva! He had to talk with her and ask her forgiveness. He picked up the phone and dialed her mother's home. Eva answered the phone.

"Eva, I'm sorry," began Harold, "I don't blame you for never wanting to see me again. But Eva, I want you home more than anything else. I'm going to try—really try not to fail you again. Please, bring the kids and come home."

Harold waited for her answer, praying. After a long silence, she spoke, "You had better go on to work, Harold. Then the girls and I will come home."[3]

That evening when Harold pulled into the driveway, he could see the warm glow of lights on inside. He felt a strange mixture of happiness and shame as he walked in. After putting the girls to bed, Eva and Harold kindled a fire in the fireplace for the first time in ages. They sat together and talked until late into the night. Harold couldn't bring himself to tell Eva about the gun, but he shared with her

The old fears about his drinking problem began to assert themselves. But he knew this time things were different. He had had an encounter with the Living God.

how he believed God had changed him.

He knew he couldn't expect Eva to renew her trust in him overnight; that would take some time. However, that evening they began the long journey to rebuild their marriage and family.

The next evening after dinner, Harold took the family Bible from the bookcase and opened it. As he sat there reading, his two young daughters, Connie and Carol, timidly approached him. They had come to kiss him goodnight.

Harold choked back his tears as he embraced them. It was

with sadness that he realized how he had missed out giving and receiving affection from his precious daughters.

When they left for bed, his thoughts returned to the Bible on his lap. He remembered a verse he learned in childhood: "I will repay you for the years that the swarming locust has eaten" (Joel 2:25). He thought of the wasted years—could God really bring a blessing from them? He closed the Bible meditatively, redoubling his commitment and resting in what had been promised through the word.

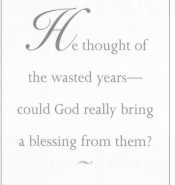

He thought of the wasted years—could God really bring a blessing from them?

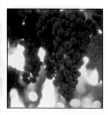

Since that evening, the Lord indeed restored the years that the locusts had eaten. Harold experienced complete deliverance from addiction to alcohol and enjoyed the restoration of his marriage and family. Six years later, Harold Hughes was elected to the state commerce commission. It was the beginning of a distinguished career in public service that culminated in his election to the office of governor of the state of Iowa.

Harold Hughes is a man whose failure and accompanying guilt brought him to the end of his tether. His story illustrates the fact that self-condemnation rarely leads to a positive resolution of our problems. It is not enough to focus on what we may or may not have done wrong: It takes a Higher Power to pull us out of the valley of despair.

Looking back, Harold realizes that his drinking problem was only an external symptom that masked underlying emotional difficulties that stemmed from his earlier military service. He was raised in a Christian home where he was taught that it was wrong to kill.

Harold spent 14 long, hard months in combat during World War II in North Africa and in Sicily. He fought to establish the Anzio beachhead before almost dying in a military hospital from a combination of malaria and jaundice. After his discharge, disturbed by his guilt about having to kill in the war, Harold sought solace in alcohol.

Mercifully, Harold was given the divine grace to reach out to God in his darkest hour. And so it is with everyone: It is sadly true that we often do not seek divine help until the situation becomes so utterly hopeless that

there is no possibility we can solve the problem ourselves. But God desires our fellowship at all times, not just when we need his help. As we read in the Psalms: "Do not be like the horse or the mule, without understanding, whose temper must be curbed with bit and bridle, else it will not stay near you" (Psalm 32:9).

As the horse's bridle compels it to pay attention to its master, life's crises often serve the purpose of drawing us closer to our Creator. But we shouldn't have to wait until the bottom drops out before we commune with the One who loves us and cares for us.

Part II:

Why Do Bad Things Happen?

As he walked along, he saw a man blind from birth. His disciples asked him, "Rabbi, who sinned, this man or his parents, that he was born blind?" Jesus answered, "Neither this man nor his parents sinned; he was born blind so that God's works might be revealed in him. We must work the works of him who sent me while it is day; night is coming when no one can work. As long as I am in the world, I am the light of the world."

John 9:1-5

Healing Through the Power of Prayer

CHAPTER 7: The Sources of Sickness

> Jesus answered, "Neither this man nor his parents sinned; he was born blind so that God's works might be revealed in him."
>
> John 9:3

On Mount Moriah in Jerusalem stands one of the most imposing buildings of the ancient world: A massive structure called the Temple Mount towers above the Kidron Valley. Its area covers a quarter of the ancient city. The temple that Jesus knew was called the

Second Temple. (The first—built by Solomon— was destroyed by the Babylonians in 586 B.C.) Herod the Great reconstructed this monumental edifice as much a lasting tribute to himself as to the God of his Jewish subjects.

And last it did. As prophesied by Jesus, the temple itself was destroyed by the Romans in A.D. 70. The immense foundation and retaining wall, however, have withstood the ravages of time and continue to dominate the vista of the Old

City. Tour guides point out the colossal limestone blocks, some of which are 40 feet in length and weigh as many tons. They are joined so masterfully, without cement, that even today a piece of paper cannot be slipped between many of the blocks.

It was on the broad expanse of the temple grounds—where today hordes of pilgrims tread—that Jesus once again encountered the hostility of the religious establishment. The Gospel of John records how after one of his visits to the temple, "they picked up stones to throw at him, but Jesus hid himself and went out of the temple" (John 8:59).

After he left the temple, an incident occurred that will serve as a springboard for our discussion of the causes of sickness: "As he walked along, he saw a man blind from birth. His disciples asked him, 'Rabbi,

who sinned, this man or his parents, that he was born blind?' Jesus answered, 'Neither this man nor his parents sinned; he was born blind so that God's works might be revealed in him'" (John 9:1–3). Jesus then sent the man to the nearby Pool of Siloam to wash, and the man was healed.

The disciples' question is a curious one. We might understand someone being struck blind for a wrong they themselves have committed. We might even comprehend someone being born blind because of the sin of his parents. Drug abuse by a pregnant mother, for example, can cause birth defects, and some venereal diseases can cause blindness in newborn infants. But how can someone be born blind as the result of sins they

Healing Through the Power of Prayer

themselves committed before they were born?

My Will Be Done

One explanation comes to mind as to why the disciples would even ask such a thing: The religious thought—or worldview—of the East had influenced the culture of first-century Palestine. This is certainly a possibility since centuries earlier Alexander the Great had conquered the then-known world that stretched to the Indus Valley. We can easily imagine a cross-fertilization of ideas spreading to the Middle East, which the Greeks occupied before the rise of the Roman Empire.

A central doctrine of Eastern Mysticism is that of reincarnation, the belief that souls experience continual rebirths in their quest for perfection. To the Eastern mind, the disciples' question would make perfect sense. And the answer would also be clear: Physical imperfections are the result of wrongs—or negative Karma—committed in a previous lifetime.

People, it is believed, willingly re-enter the cycle of life and experience sickness and pain to achieve a spiritual goal. Indeed, for the Eastern worldview there can be no other explanation; the Law of Karma is unalterable.

Thus infirmity is looked upon as a self-imposed limitation that we somehow "will" on ourselves (whether or not we are consciously aware of having done so). Many meditation and visualization techniques are based on the premise that we—not a God existing outside of ourselves—create our own reality.

But this can lead to a callous attitude towards the individual who cannot seem to will their way to health. Dr. David

Spiegel, of Stanford University School of Medicine, relates an example of cold insensitivity toward a patient of his who had become seriously ill: "[A] woman in our [cancer support] group, a brilliant woman who wrote books on computer programming, had ... gone to get special training in visualization techniques. When she came back and learned that her disease had spread substantially, she called a counselor from the imagery group, who said to her, 'Why did you want your cancer to spread?' Fortunately, she was strong enough to tell him to go to hell. But many patients are afflicted with this burden of guilt, that if you can't control the course of disease, it must be your fault."[1]

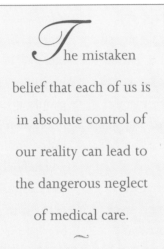

The mistaken belief that each of us is in absolute control of our reality can lead to the dangerous neglect of medical care.

While Dossey himself is an advocate for the Eastern worldview, in his own medical practice he has seen the self-blame it produces: "'If only I'd been farther along my spiritual path, the biopsy would have come back negative,' one of my patients once said. Why do we blame ourselves for getting sick? I call this New Age guilt, and it is currently epidemic in our society."[2]

The mistaken belief that each one of us is in absolute control of our reality can also lead to the dangerous neglect of medical care, as occurred in another case cited by Spiegel:

Healing Through the Power of Prayer

"A woman in our [psychological support] group was also attending a group in which she visualized her cancer cells being eaten by her leukocyte [white blood] cells. She decided not only to drop out of our group but also to stop receiving chemotherapy and radiation. We argued vigorously with her not to do that. I said, 'If you want to visualize, visualize, but stay with your medical treatment.' She quit anyway, and was dead within a year."[3]

Such are the pitfalls of deceiving ourselves that we have somehow "chosen" our illness in some pre-existent state and can thus "unchoose" it at will. Dr. Borysenko, another advocate for the Eastern worldview, realizes its inherent limitations. She describes her reaction at a mind/body conference where one of the speakers "tried to convince the audience that spiritual awakening is a sure-fire cure for illness. I could feel my blood start to boil as he went on and on about spirituality and perfect health."

Finally she could take it no longer: "I stood up and challenged the speaker who, to me, represented a subtle, dangerous type of New Age Gestapo member. I explained that he was unleashing terror on people, giving them the impression that illness is . . . the badge of the unenlightened. I pointed out that all the mystics and spiritual teachers were dead, many of cancer. Upon hearing this protestation the entire audience sprang to their feet and gave me a standing ovation."

In a classic instance of the attitude "if the facts contradict me then the facts are wrong," Borysenko tells how the speaker sought her out after the session. He attempted to con-

Healing Through the Power of Prayer

vince her that the gurus she had cited really weren't enlightened after all.[4]

There is yet another difficulty with the Eastern view: If sickness is self-imposed for some spiritual purpose, then to try to heal infirmity would be to interfere with the "divine purpose." In fact, hindering the working out of someone's Karma in this way might do more harm than good because they could not accomplish their spiritual goals for that particular lifetime.

This is not merely an interesting question for philosophers to debate: We can also see how this fatalistic attitude works out in practice. Belief in reincarnation provided the justification for a country like India keeping those in the lower castes (who are supposedly less-advanced spiritually) in a state of abject poverty. Historically, it was only until the influence, however imperfect, of the British in the nineteenth-century that social and medical services along with a semblance of equal opportunity for the poor began to take root.

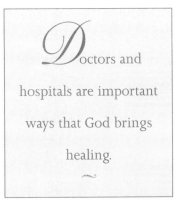

Doctors and hospitals are important ways that God brings healing.

Doctors and hospitals are important ways that God brings healing. But the idea that each individual—whether aware of it or not—is in absolute control of their "reality" and bodily condition renders the need for medical assistance unnecessary. This illusion can have dangerous consequences if people don't seek the medical help

Healing Through the Power of Prayer

they need. Dossey tells the story of a woman named Carol, who he describes as one of his healthiest patients. Carol prided herself on "'taking full responsibility' for her health and for 'consciously creating [her] own reality'—100 percent!"

Dossey relates how late one evening he was summoned to the emergency room only to be surprised to find Carol lying on a stretcher, very near death.[5] Tests

revealed that her appendix had ruptured. She was taken to surgery, and fortunately the diseased appendix was successfully removed.

Dossey was baffled as to why someone as "in tune" with herself as Carol ignored the warning symptoms and waited so long before seeking medical help. A few days later he had the opportunity to ask her why she hadn't called him. "Immediately she began to sob. Finally she managed to say through her tears, 'Because I was so ashamed! I felt like a complete failure!' Carol's heroic task of fashioning her reality through her conscious efforts had failed. Her

> *A*ttempting to convince ourselves that we create our own reality can only lead to guilt and a sense of failure when the inevitable occurs and reality fails to cooperate with our wishful thinking.

Healing Through the Power of Prayer

world had crumbled and lay in shambles all about her."[6]

Attempting to convince ourselves that we create our own reality can only lead to guilt and a sense of failure when the inevitable occurs and reality fails to cooperate with our wishful thinking. A power much greater than ourselves is ultimately in control of what happens to us.

THE UNPARDONABLE SIN

Jesus' succinct reply "Neither" puts an end to speculation as to whether the blind man or his parents were responsible for his being born sightless. He did not will himself to be born blind to redress negative Karma from a previous lifetime.

If we ourselves do not choose to become sick, then how or why does it happen? Tom Harpur describes this cry

of the soul for understanding: "When you spend time with people during their moments of crisis, when they or those very close to them are seriously ill in body and spirit, there is one cry you hear over and over again: Why did this happen? What did I (or they) do wrong? Behind this poignant cri de coeur are a couple of assumptions: that illness is a form of punishment, and that it is sent by God."[7]

It is vital to recognize that shock, anger, and protestations to God in the midst of a severe trial are normal and to be expected. We need only look to Jesus' heartrending words while on the cross: "My God, My God, why have you forsaken me?" (Mark 15:33).

For the one and only time of his eternal existence, Jesus

Healing Through the Power of Prayer

experienced on the cross the awful sense of separation from his Father because the sins of the world had been placed upon him. His cry reflects his sense of abandonment, just as we also may sometimes feel that God is not tuned in to our particular crises.

The Psalms are full of complaints directed toward God in the midst of suffering:

"All this has come upon us,
  yet we have not forgotten
    you,
  or been false to your
    covenant.
Our heart has not turned back,
  nor have our steps departed
    from your way,
  yet you have broken us in the
    haunt of jackals,
  and covered us with deep
    darkness. . . .
Rouse yourself! Why do you
    sleep, O Lord?
  Awake, do not cast us off
    forever!

Why do you hide your face?
  Why do you forget our
    affliction and oppression?"
(Psalm 44:17–19,23–24).

Many Christians assume that adopting the proper "spiritual" attitude toward life's trials means putting on a phony smile and banning all negative speech from conversation. How refreshing it is to read a psalm such as this one, written to assist us in our own prayers! The psalmist here is not taking a pseudospiritual approach to his trials, but rather is expressing his honest emotions.

There are those who fear they have committed the "Unpardonable Sin" when, in the midst of pain and suffering, they found themselves railing against or even cursing God. But God knows our human frailties and takes them into consideration:

"Yet he, being compassionate,
  forgave their iniquity,

and did not destroy them...
He remembered that they were
    but flesh,
    a wind that passes and does
        not come again"
(Psalm 78:38–39).

God is more concerned with our inward attitude toward him than what we may say in a moment or period of extreme frustration. We are assured that "the Lord does not see as mortals see; they look on the outward appearance, but the Lord looks on the heart" (1 Samuel 16:7). Indeed, it has been well said that the one who is sincerely troubled about having committed the Unpardonable Sin most assuredly has

> *W*e are assured
> that "the Lord does not
> see as mortals see;
> they look on the
> outward appearance,
> but the Lord looks on
> the heart.
>
> *1 Samuel 16:7*

not. That is because by their disquiet they are exhibiting the continuing presence of the Holy Spirit in their life.

But we must now address a thorny question: Does God directly send sickness into our lives? Some, like Harpur, are adamant that he does not: "Sickness is not a divine punishment nor is it sent as a lesson or as a means of purifying character. Such a view would make a sadistic monster out of God instead of the loving source of light and energy revealed by Christ."[8]

Is this view expressed by Harpur correct? We must first make it plain that God is not a

Healing Through the Power of Prayer

cruel, vindictive potentate who gets his kicks out of torturing his poor subjects. Nor must we assume that when someone becomes ill that it is the result of their sinfulness. As we have already observed in the example of Job, it is very possible for the innocent to suffer terribly.

GOD COULDN'T HELP IT

But is the opposite view then correct—that sickness is never part of God's divine plan for our life? This is the position taken by Rabbi Harold Kushner in his thought-provoking book *Why Bad Things Happen to Good People*. Kushner wrote the book in an attempt to understand the death of his son. He could not accept the fact that God would directly will such a tragedy. And yet, contrary to the Rabbi's fervent hopes and prayers, his son died.

For Kushner that could only mean one thing: God was unable to prevent his son's death—and if he could not prevent it, then he could not be blamed. By abandoning his belief in the all-powerfulness of God he was able to continue to picture God as kind and loving—not as a cruel potentate who would will the death of a child.

Kushner admits that it is a difficult transition for many to think of God as less than perfect just "as it was for us, when we were children, to realize that our parents were not all-powerful, that a broken toy had to be thrown out because they *could not* fix it, not because they did not want to."[9]

It must be admitted at the onset that there is something attractive about Kushner's view of God. After all, if God is trying his best to "fix" us like our parents tried to repair our

Healing Through the Power of Prayer

broken toys, then it is hard to blame him for trying. Along with the rest of us, Kushner's God hopes for the best even though, like us, much of the time he is unable to do much about it.

But while appearing to solve one problem, Kushner's solution raises others. For one, it is hard to see what good it would do to pray to a God who is impotent and unable to alter the course of events. The act of prayer assumes that God is indeed capable of changing things for the better.

Therefore, it is not surprising that Kushner's opinion about prayer changes along with his view of God. Prayer, for him, is no longer about altering the course of events. It is, rather, about enabling us to accept whatever hand fate has dealt us: "'If God can't make my sickness go away, what good is He? Who needs Him?' God does not want you to be sick or crippled. He didn't make you have this problem, and He doesn't want you to go on having it, but He can't make it go away. That is something which is too hard even for God. What good is He, then? God makes people become doctors and nurses to try to make you feel better. . . . And in the knowledge that we are not alone, that God is one our side, we manage to go on."[10]

Kushner's book contains much wisdom and is written

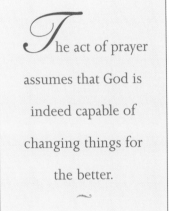

The act of prayer assumes that God is indeed capable of changing things for the better.

Healing Through the Power of Prayer

from the perspective of one who has been "in the trenches" as a rabbi serving his congregation. He also knows what it is like to suffer an overwhelming loss that words and deeds cannot assuage. He has no time for trite theological maxims that only seem to bring more pain rather than help.

Kushner focuses on the love and compassion of God, something that those who are suffering need to grasp hold of. But when we are sick and in pain, we need *more* than knowing that God is on our side. We want someone who can help. A God who hopes for the best, like any well-meaning but powerless friend, is simply not enough.

In times of distress, people need to be able to put their hope in God—to believe that he can work a miracle in their situation.

This is precisely the refrain echoed throughout the Psalms: God is all-powerful and able to help those who trust in him. "Say to God, 'How awesome are your deeds! Because of your great power, your enemies cringe before you.

All the earth worships you;
  they sing praises to you,
  sing praises to your name.'
Come and see what God has
    done:
  he is awesome in his deeds
    among mortals.

> *In times of distress, people need to be able to put their hope in God—to believe that he can work a miracle in their situation.*

There we rejoiced in him,
 who rules by his might
  forever,
 whose eyes keep watch on
  the nations. . . .
Bless our God, O peoples. . . .
who has kept us among the
  living,
 and has not let our feet slip"
(Psalm 66:3–5).

This does not sound like an impotent God. Quite the opposite. The Psalms inspire us and give us hope because they assure us that there *is* a God in heaven who is merciful and able to act on our behalf. Indeed, what a cold, dark universe it would be without a loving and all-powerful Creator.

CHAPTER 8:
The Sources of Sickness II

> "If you will listen carefully to the voice of the Lord your God, and do what is right in his sight, and give heed to his commandments and keep all his statutes, I will not bring upon you any of the diseases that I brought upon the Egyptians; for I am the Lord who heals you."
>
> Exodus 15:26

If God is all-powerful, then we cannot allow ourselves to imagine that anything happens without him permitting it. But this brings us back to Rabbi  Kushner's dilemma: If God could prevent bad things—and does not—is that evidence that he is cruel and heartless?

In an attempt to explain this question, theologians make a distinction between God's *perfect* will and his *permissive* will. God will permit things to happen to us that are not in his ideal plan for us. For example, certain adverse consequences will

Healing Through the Power of Prayer

follow if we choose to abuse our bodies with harmful drugs. While it is obviously not a part of the divine plan for us to ruin our bodies, we have been granted the freedom to make moral choices—and God respects those choices. Not to do so would in effect take away our ability to choose.

So it may be helpful to say that bad things are allowed to happen to us because of God's permissive but not his perfect will. But this opens the possibility that sickness may be the result of wrong choices we make. The Bible is clear that there are times when this is indeed the case, as in the confession of the psalmist:

"There is no soundness in my
　　flesh
　because of your indignation;
there is no health in my bones
　　because of my sin.
For my iniquities have gone
　　over my head;

they weigh
　like a
　burden
　too heavy
　for me.
My wounds grow foul and
　　fester
　because of my foolishness;
I am utterly bowed down and
　　prostrate;
　all day long I go around
　　mourning.
For my loins are filled with
　　burning,
　and there is no soundness in
　　my flesh.
I am utterly spent and crushed;
　I groan because of the tumult
　　of my heart. . . .
My friends and companions
　　stand aloof from my
　　affliction,
　and my neighbors stand far
　　off"
(Psalm 38:3–8,11).

This is by no means an isolated passage. Far from it: The Scriptures are replete with

Healing Through the Power of Prayer

examples both of individuals and of the Israelites being punished with disease because of their sin. In the Old Testament alone there are more than 50 references to disease or pestilence being the result or threatened result of sin. When the children of Israel were on their way to Sinai after the Exodus, the Lord spoke to them: "He said, 'If you will listen carefully to the voice of the Lord your God, and do what is right in his sight, and give heed to his commandments and keep all his statutes, I will not bring upon you any of the diseases that I brought upon the Egyptians; for I am the Lord who heals you'" (Exodus 15:26).

Some people are quite understandably uncomfortable with any discussion of sickness being caused by sin, because it can lead to false guilt and a judgmental attitude toward those who are sick. Morton Kelsey shows a pastoral concern for the destructive power of guilt: "Anthropologists have told of many examples of people dying when they have broken a tabu in a tabu culture of which they were an integral part. When people believe that they have incurred divine wrath in breaking what they conceive to be divine law, they can be so overcome by guilt and fear that this alone can cause mental and physical illness. The loving God revealed in Jesus of Nazareth wants to draw all people into the orbit of love, not to destroy the offender."[1]

Kelsey's point is well-taken; it is possible to heap unnecessary guilt upon ourselves that our Maker does not intend us to bear. We have been created with a conscience to warn us of wrong actions, but sometimes self-imposed guilt masquerades as our conscience. An example of this would be a woman who feels guilty whenever she spends money on herself, even when her need for clothing and personal items is perfectly justifiable. Her (false) guilt may stem from seeing pictures of impoverished people around the world who have much less than she does. Or her feelings of guilt may come from a strict upbringing by parents who taught her that it was wrong to spend money that could be saved. A pastor or wise counselor can help us discern what is false guilt from what might be genuine guilt.

Telling someone what we think are the sinful causes of their illness can have a devastating effect. Kushner relates the story of a young pharmacist named Ron. One night when Ron was preparing to close up the store, a teenage drug addict entered, pulled out a gun, and demanded drugs and money. Ron knew that his life was more valuable than anything in the store and willingly complied. But when he tried to open the cash register, his hands started trembling from fear. As he reached for the counter to brace himself, the robber thought he was going for a gun and shot him. The bullet lodged in his spine and, despite the efforts of the surgeons, Ron was paralyzed for life.

In a misguided attempt at comforting him, an acquaintance tried to tell Ron why God

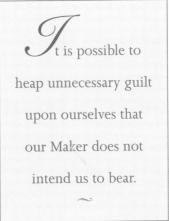

It is possible to heap unnecessary guilt upon ourselves that our Maker does not intend us to bear.

Healing Through the Power of Prayer

allowed him to become paralyzed: "'Look at it this way,' said his friend, 'You were always a pretty cocky guy, popular with girls, flashy cars, confident you were going to make a lot of money. You never really took time to worry about the people who couldn't keep up with you. Maybe this is God's way of teaching you a lesson, making you more thoughtful, more sensitive to others.'"[2]

Perhaps we should ask who needed to work on being sensitive to others—Ron or his friend. Comfort like this can be devastating to someone in the throes of a physical calamity. We are reminded of Job's anguished response to what he calls his "miserable comforters":

"I also could talk as you do,
   if you were in my place;
I could join words together
      against you,
   and shake my head at you.

I could encourage you with my
      mouth,
   and the solace of my lips
      would assuage your pain"
(Job 16:4–5).

We should never put ourselves in the place of God and pass judgment on why sickness or tragedy has occurred in someone's life. While the possibility always exists that sickness is the result of sinful behavior, that is something only God knows and only God can judge. Ron knew as much, and says he was only restrained by his infirmity from punching his friend.

It is only human to want a ready explanation why people suffer tragedies and illness. How many of us have secretly, in our heart of hearts, wondered: "They must have done something to deserve that!"

We allow thoughts like that because it is natural to want an easy explanation for why people suffer difficulties. It

Healing Through the Power of Prayer

relieves us of our responsibility to show pity or empathize with the suffering individual. They are, after all, only receiving their just rewards.

We find in the Gospel of Luke one occasion when Jesus addresses the issue of whether tragedies are the direct result of sinful behavior. Christ was told about a group called the Galileans "whose blood Pilate had mingled with their sacrifices." Jesus then said, "Do you think that because these Galileans suffered in this way they were worse sinners than all other Galileans? No, I tell you; but unless you repent, you will all perish as they did. Or those eighteen who were killed when the tower in Siloam fell on them—do you think that they were worse offenders than all the others living in Jerusalem? No, I tell you; but unless you repent, you will all perish just as they did" (Luke 13:2–5).

The answer to our question about the relationship between sin and sickness could scarcely be stated more clearly. Yes, the possibility always exists that our misfortunes are caused by sin, and each of us has an obligation to examine our hearts. But—and this is Jesus' point—even when we are guilty of sin, we are no more sinful than other people.

> *We should never put ourselves in the place of God and pass judgment on why sickness or tragedy has occurred in someone's life.*

Healing Through the Power of Prayer

As we examine the healings recorded in the gospels, we find that the primary focus of Jesus is not on the person's sin: "When he saw a need to speak of sin in connection with a healing, he did not say that this was the sole cause of the person's trouble. Jesus seemed to believe that a primary cause of sickness was a force of evil loose in the world which was hostile to God and the divine way. He believed that people sometimes fell into the hands of this power, which then exerted a destructive influence in their lives, morally, psychologically, and physically."[3]

If Jesus did not focus on sin as a cause of illness, neither should we. That should be left for God alone to judge.

AN ERRANT DESTRUCTIVENESS

Kelsey describes a potent cause of human suffering—the existence of evil: "You may call this force Satan, the devil, evil spirits, demons, autonomous complexes, or what you will; its exact source was never fully accounted for. But this understanding, this knowledge of the reality of such errant destructiveness is shot through the teaching and actions of Jesus."[4]

It is fashionable even in religious circles to downplay the existence of objective evil in the world around us. Cartoon images contribute to our agnosticism by picturing the devil as a comical figure with pitchfork and forked tail. Surely, we imagine, such a concept belongs to medieval superstition rather than the modern world.

It seems not to have occurred to those who take this view that this is precisely how the Evil One would like them to think. Pope John Paul II has spoken of the reality of the evil spiritual personage the Bible calls Satan: "To conclude, we must add that the impressive words of the Apostle John, 'The whole world lies under the power of the evil one' (1 John 5:19), allude also the presence of Satan in the history of humanity, a presence which becomes all the more acute when man and society depart from God. The influence of the evil spirit can conceal itself in a more profound and effective way: it is in his 'interests' to make himself unknown. Satan has the skill to deny his existence in the name of rationalism and of every other system of thought which seeks all possible means to avoid recognizing his activity.

This, however, does not signify the elimination of man's free will and responsibility, and even less the frustration of the saving action of Christ. It is, rather, a case of a conflict between the dark powers of evil and the power of redemption."[5]

It is no exaggeration to say that, directly or indirectly, the root of everything bad that happens to us can ultimately be traced back to the activity of the Evil One in the Garden of Eden. Refusing to accept the reality of an evil force in the world flies in the face of the evidence. How else can we possibly explain the horrors that we witness on a daily basis through television and newspapers?

If Jesus did not focus on sin as a cause of illness, neither should we. That should be left for God alone to judge.

Healing Through the Power of Prayer

The Apostle Paul informs us that since the disobedience of the first man, Adam, the deadly virus of sin has spread to all humankind: "Therefore, just as sin came into the world through one man, and death came through sin, and so death spread to all because all have sinned" (Romans 5:12).

And it is not only humankind but creation itself that seeks deliverance from its "bondage to decay" (Romans 8:21). There was no sickness, no death, before the Fall into sin. We read in Genesis that the pain of childbirth, the curse of the ground itself, and the "painful toil" of labor by the sweat of one's brow became a reality only after the Garden. The Fall unleashed a torrent of  harmful consequences that has spread to every aspect of our exis-tence on earth. Doubtless, all manner of harmful bacteria, viruses, and disease came into existence after the loss of innocence in Eden. That, in short, is why we get sick and die.

The presence of sin also means that individuals will make wrong and harmful choices that will impact not only themselves but others. The sinful consequences of a drunk driver who runs a red light, causing a deadly accident, spread like a shock wave to complete strangers. The drug company that, wary of financial loss, attempts to cover up evidence linking their product with cancer may inflict a deadly disease upon many. And the dictator whose military aggression leads to war sends waves of young men to an early death.

In perhaps none of these catastrophes, whether natural or wrought by human hands, are the afflicted guilty of what

Healing Through the Power of Prayer

is causing them to suffer and die. The traffic fatality may have been a model of sobriety; the cancer victim a person of high integrity; and the soldier a man of peace. They died because the effects of the Fall have permeated the world. Since no person is an island, they could not escape the inevitable.

The Apostle Paul understood the underlying cause of evil in the world and describes this state of affairs in terms of a cosmic confrontation: "For our struggle is not against enemies of flesh and blood, but against the rulers, against the authorities, against the cosmic powers of this present darkness, against the spiritual forces of evil in the heavenly places. Therefore take up the full armor of God, so that you may be able to withstand on that evil day, and having done everything, to stand firm" (Ephesians 6:12–13).

The presence of sin in the world also means that individuals will make wrong and harmful choices that will impact not only themselves but others.

The bad news is that we are up against a potent enemy that outclasses us at every turn. The good news is that a mighty ally has weighed in on our side. Jesus came to bring the kingdom of God to earth. But before that could be accomplished, the kingdom of Satan had to be overturned.

Healing Through the Power of Prayer

Jesus' earthly ministry constituted an assault upon the spiritual strongholds of evil.

Sickness and disease were viewed by the people of Jesus' day as signs of bondage to the forces of evil. Thus, one way of demonstrating his purpose for coming to earth was to break the hold of Satan and his forces through healing. The Gospel of Matthew describes how Jesus waged war against evil: "Jesus went throughout Galilee, teaching in their synagogues and proclaiming the good news of the kingdom and curing every disease and every sickness among the people. So his fame spread throughout all Syria, and they brought to him all the sick, those who were afflicted with various diseases and pains, demoniacs, epileptics, and paralytics, and he cured them" (Matthew 4:23–24).

Healings accompanied Jesus' preaching about the coming of his kingdom. They constituted practical, indisputable proof of his power over the Evil One. In one example that illustrates his desire to liberate people from the power of Satan, Jesus defends his healing of a chronically handicapped woman despite objections that he should not heal on the Sabbath: "And ought not this woman, a daughter of Abraham whom Satan bound for eighteen long years, be set free from this bondage on the sabbath day?" (Luke 13:16).

Here again we see that Jesus was not focusing on any sin the woman might have committed. His intention was to free her from the powers of darkness that had enslaved her.

ANOTHER LOOK

We have scarcely begun to plumb the depths of the subject of why bad things happen to us. This is by no means a purely academic discussion: It is a profoundly personal question that will sooner or later touch all of us.

The first observation that can be made is that Jesus does not entertain the Eastern worldview—that bad things are leftover Karma from previous lifetimes and that each person creates their own reality. Sooner or later this view is doomed to failure.

If the mystics of Eastern religions were unable to prevent sickness from happening, what hope is there for the rest of us? Part of the answer is to avoid self-delusion. It goes without saying that each of us needs to do our best to take care of our bodies and minds so as to prevent illness. But, we are often powerless either to prevent illness or to heal ourselves.

Our second observation is that the view that God is as powerless as we are to heal offers scant comfort to those who are suffering. Indeed, it is difficult to conceive of a God without the power to change things. There would be no more reason to pray to this God than we would pray to, for example, a kindly uncle. At least the kindly uncle might give us a modest stipend to help out with expenses.

The Bible presents a picture of God as all-powerful. Even so,

> "*A*nd ought not this woman, a daughter of Abraham whom Satan bound for eighteen long years, be set free from this bondage on the sabbath day?"
>
> Luke 13:16

Healing Through the Power of Prayer

there is one important sense in which God's power is limited: We have been granted the freedom to choose and God cannot change the choices we make. He can, and does, forgive us when we ask his forgiveness for a wrong decision; he can mitigate the consequences for those who repent; but he cannot force us to do what is right. We are not automatons. If God controls our decisions, then we are not truly free to choose.

It is in this sense that we can agree with Kushner that God cannot forcibly change the intent of evil in a human's heart that so often leads to tragedy. If a person determines to commit a heinous crime, God will not always restrain him. We know this is true because many horrible crimes are committed. Nevertheless, God will sometimes prevent the crime from being committed for the sake of the

innocent, as illustrated by news accounts of a dramatic confrontation that occurred some years ago.

In the incident, a woman driving on interstate highway 57 near Kankakee, Illinois, was forced onto the shoulder by two men on a murder and robbery spree that eventually claimed three victims. When ordered into the men's car, the woman calmly looked at them and said, "God will protect me."

The woman then got back in her own car and drove away unhindered. One cannot help but believe that this woman's life was spared because God honored her when she called upon his name. Beyond this we cannot venture. We do not know if any of the other victims also prayed, or why so many others are not also rescued from evil.

To say that God is unjust in not preventing tragedy is to

Healing Through the Power of Prayer

make a judgment that is beyond our capacity as human beings to render, for only a being the equal of God would be capable of judging him. The same idea is embodied in the legal right to a "trial by our peers." But who is a "peer" of God, who can see every extenuating circumstance and foresee all possible future ramifications of any given situation? Truly we "see in a mirror, dimly."

It is better to pray than not to pray. Even though we have no assurance that our prayers will be answered as we would want them to be, at least the possibility exists that they may be. And if they are not answered as we would wish, then we can, perhaps not without great struggle, choose to believe and understand that there *is* a purpose, unknown to us, in our suffering.

> *E*ven though we have no assurance that our prayers will be answered as we would want them to be, at least the possibility exists that they may be.

Third, we must always be willing to consider the possibility that our misfortune is the result of our own actions. For the heavy smoker, lung cancer may be the price he pays for abusing his body. And, as we have already seen, medical researchers believe that harmful mental attitudes such as anger, stress, and anxiety can trigger physical illness.

The Bible also indicates that wrong behavior can cause sick-

Healing Through the Power of Prayer

ness. The Apostle Paul mentions this possibility when discussing abuses in the Corinthian church related to the Lord's Supper: "Examine yourselves, and only then eat of the bread and drink of the cup. For all who eat and drink without discerning the body, eat and drink judgment against themselves. For this reason many of you are weak and ill, and some have died" (1 Corinthians 11:28–30).

But at the same time, we must be careful. We cannot assume in every case that sickness is the direct result of sin. This can lead to an attitude of self-condemnation, as Kushner relates in a story that occurred when he was a young rabbi just starting out in his profession. He was called upon to comfort a family who had just suffered a terrible loss. Their only child, a 19-year-old daughter who was a freshman in college, collapsed and died one morning while walking to class.

Kushner, at a loss for words and not knowing what to expect, arrived at their home the same day. He anticipated having to explain why God would take their only child. Instead, he was astonished to hear the grieving parents blame themselves. In their very first words to him they confessed that they had not fasted the previous Yom Kippur.

As Kushner writes, the only explanation that presented itself to the parents was that somehow they had displeased God: "They sat there feeling that their daughter's death had been their fault; had they been less selfish and less lazy about the Yom Kippur fast some six months earlier, she might still be alive. They sat there angry at God for having exacted his pound of flesh so strictly, but afraid to admit their anger for fear that He would punish them again."[6]

This approach is unsatisfactory. There are cases where a direct causal relationship can be seen between our actions and the resultant bad effect—such as smoking cigarettes and lung cancer. But apart from cases like these, there is no way for us to know—short of divine revelation—what sin caused what bad thing in our lives. Unless we have real reasons to suspect a direct causal relationship, we should abandon the attempt to discern why the bad thing happened to us.

Our fourth conclusion is that in many cases sickness and tragedies happen because of the existence of objective evil in the world. The Bible warns us about this evil and describes it as a personal force: "Discipline yourselves, keep alert. Like a roaring lion your adversary the devil prowls around, looking for someone to devour. Resist him, steadfast in your faith" (1 Peter 5:8–9).

We can understand, though not condone, the motivation behind some forms of evil, such as the individual who steals out of poverty: "Thieves are not despised who steal only to satisfy their appetite when they are hungry. Yet if they are caught, they will pay sevenfold;

We must be careful. We cannot assume in every case that sickness is the direct result of sin. This can lead to an attitude of self-condemnation.

Healing Through the Power of Prayer

they will forfeit all the goods of their house" (Proverbs 6:30–31).

But evil also takes other monstrous forms, which some of us have directly experienced or at the least read about or watched with mouth agape on the television screen. Pictures of serial killers, senseless drive-by killings, and the bloody slaughter of third-world strife assault our senses unmercifully. When it comes to understanding the motivation behind such cases, the psychologists and sociologists fail us.

To downplay such depravity is tantamount to a slap in the face for its victims. The only sufficient explanation for such raw, brutal, wholly incomprehensible violence is the existence of deliberate, malignant evil in the world, which drives people to such unspeakable actions.

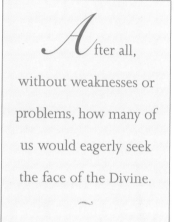

After all, without weaknesses or problems, how many of us would eagerly seek the face of the Divine.

According to the Bible, sin and evil have not only infected every man and woman, but have brought about a process of disintegration in Creation itself. Thus we cannot avoid the process of physical decay that leads to sickness and death.

But that is not the end of the story. The evil who threatens to overwhelm the world and all that are in it will ultimately fail, as Paul promises: "The God of peace will shortly crush Satan under your feet" (Romans 16:20). The victory of God through Christ over the powers of darkness extends to our own healing: "He himself bore our sins in his body on the cross, so that, free from sins, we might live for righteousness; by his wounds you have been healed" (1 Peter 2:24).

There is a fifth and final clue as to the reason behind suffering and illness, and for this we must return once again to the story of the man born blind. According to Jesus, he was born blind to reveal the "work of God in his life." That is, his infirmity provided the occasion for a demonstration of the power and the presence of God. After all, without weaknesses or problems, how many of us would eagerly seek the face of the Divine? To be sure, we may not be cognizant of what the "work of God" in one's life is—and that certainly contributes to our frustration. But we should always be aware that there is a greater divine purpose in sickness and adversity.

We now have some basis for understanding why bad things happen.

Part III:

How to Pray for Healing

As he approached the gate of the town, a
man who had died was being carried out.
He was his mother's only son, and she was
a widow; and with her was a large crowd
from the town. When the Lord saw her, he
had compassion for her and said to her,
"Do not weep." Then he came forward and
touched the bier, and the bearers stood
still. And he said, "Young man, I say to you,
rise!" The dead man sat up and began to
speak, and Jesus gave him to his mother.

Luke 7:11-15

Healing Through the Power of Prayer

CHAPTER 9:
A Tale of Two Villages

> "So I say to you, Ask, and it will be given you; search, and you will find; knock, and the door will be opened for you."
>
> Luke 11:9

The view from Mount Tabor is one of the most spectacular in all of Israel. Standing on the summit of the traditional site of the transfiguration of Christ, one looks out over a veritable panorama of biblical history. To the south, the heights of Mount Gilboa rise, framing the northern reaches of the broadest and most fertile valley in the land. There, at the foot of Gilboa by a

spring that can still be seen, is where Gideon encamped before delivering Israel from the Midionites. Later, Saul met his end here in a futile bid against the Philistines.

In the distance, barely discernible in the haze on the back slopes of the Carmel range, lies the ancient site of Megiddo, which lends its name to the valley before us. Megiddo also gives its name to the most celebrated battle yet to be, for in the Hebrew language

Armageddon means "mountain of Megiddo." Napoleon once stood here and proclaimed the site an ideal location for just such a battle.

Across the valley from Megiddo is where the opening shots of another battle were fired 2,000 years ago—the victory of the kingdom of God over the forces of evil. Mount Nazareth rises from the northern edge of the valley, nestling in its bosom the tiny village, of the same name, where Jesus grew up.

But it is to a hillock in the foreground below us, not far from the foot of Mount Tabor, that our attention is drawn. Here, on the hill called Moreh, is where the village of Endor was located. It is to the witch of Endor that a frightened and spent Saul went concealed on his last fateful night (see 1 Samuel 27). And it is here, at the hill of Moreh, that two of

the most dramatic healings recorded in the Bible occurred, separated by nearly 1,000 years.

The miracles transpired in two tiny villages on opposite sides of the hill—in Nain and in Shunem. The one facing Tabor bears the same name today as recorded in the biblical text: "Soon afterwards he went to a town called Nain, and his disciples and a large crowd went with him. As he approached the gate of the town, a man who had died was being carried out. He was his mother's only son, and she was a widow; and with her was a large crowd from the town. When the Lord saw her, he had compassion for her and said, 'Do not weep.' Then he came forward and touched the bier, and the bearers stood still. And he said, 'Young man, I say to

Healing Through the Power of Prayer

you, rise!" The dead man sat up and began to speak, and Jesus gave him to his mother" (Luke 7:11–15).

Jesus performed no more dramatic miracle, no greater demonstration of his power and authority, than raising people from the dead. Yet we find only a few instances recorded in the gospels.

In this particular healing, as in so many others, we catch a glimpse of the heart of Jesus: "When the Lord saw her, he had compassion for her." As we wrestle with the question of why bad things happen and why some people are healed and some are not, we should not lose sight of God's compassion. God does understand our pain.

Nain was one of dozens of villages in Galilee that Jesus passed through. While only a few hours walk across the valley from Nazareth, there is no indication that he knew the widow of Nain or her son. And yet his heart was touched, and he was moved to comfort her.

Saying "Do not weep," was a surprising thing to express to a mourner in the midst of a funeral procession. In the West, many of us suppress our emotions during times of grief; not

> *As we wrestle with the question of why bad things happen and why some people are healed and some are not, we should not lose sight of the compassion of God.*

so in the Middle East. If the family could not muster enough of the requisite emotions, professional mourners were hired to fill the air with wailing.

But Jesus had other plans for this funeral. Another aspect of the miracle at Nain tells us something about how Jesus healed. That is, nowhere in this story do we read of anyone asking Jesus to heal the young man. There are times when it is important to take the initiative and request prayer for ourselves and others. However, God's mysterious ways are beyond our comprehension, and in this case a miracle was performed without the person—or anyone else—having requested it.

There may be times when we hesitate to intercede for someone who shows little interest in praying themselves. We should not let that deter us from praying for their healing.

As we see from this instance, as well as others in the gospels, miracles sometimes occur without the individual's knowledge or active participation. Jesus does not wait for a formal request for his assistance. His heart of compassion reaches out to all those who are needy.

The text of Luke continues describing the incident: "Fear seized all of them; and they glorified God, saying, 'A great prophet has risen among us!' and 'God has looked favorably on his people!' This word about him spread throughout Judea and all the surrounding country" (verses 16–17).

The cry of the people of Nain that a "great prophet has risen among us" was not a common exclamation of the times. The spectacular miracle that they had just witnessed stirred an ancient memory within them, for this was not the only time that someone had been raised from the dead on the hill of Moreh. Many hundreds of years earlier, another prophet had performed a similar miracle on the other side of the knoll in Shunem.

The Shunammite Woman's Son

There exists to this day a village in the same geographic location as Nain, called Shunem. This biblical town was a way station for the journeys of the prophet Elisha. In those days—and today in the Middle East—houses were not gabled but flat, and in the hot summertime people would often sleep on the roof to enjoy the cool evening breezes.

A woman in this village of Shunem built the prophet a room on the roof of her house so he could have a place to rest when he passed through the area. In gratitude, Elisha performed the first of his miracles for the woman, who was childless. Her joy over the gift of a son, however, turned to despair years later when the young boy suddenly died. The woman hastened to find Elisha: "When she came to the man of God at the mountain, she caught hold of his feet. Gehazi [Elisha's servant] approached to push her away. But the man of God said, 'Let her alone, for she is in bitter distress; the Lord has hidden it from me and has not told me.' Then she said, 'Did I ask my lord for a son? Did I not say, Do not mislead me?'" (2 Kings 4:27–28).

The cry of the Shunammite woman echoes what many have voiced when what they thought was a blessing turned to tragedy. We hear the lament of a woman abandoned by her husband: "Why did you give me a husband in the first place? I would have been better off without him!"; or perhaps that of a man who loses his job: "I should never have gotten this job in the first place! Why did you answer my prayers when I first applied for the job if you knew what would happen?"

These are tough questions with no easy answers. Elisha does not attempt to answer the Shunammite woman's complaint. Instead, he wastes no time in going to the boy: "When Elisha came into the house, he saw the child lying dead on his bed. So he went in and closed the door on the two of them, and prayed to the Lord. Then he got up on the bed and lay upon the child, putting his mouth upon his mouth, his eyes upon his eyes, and his hands upon his hands; and while he lay bent over him, the flesh of the child became warm. He got down, walked once to and fro in the room, then got up again and bent over him; the child sneezed seven times, and the child opened his eyes. Elisha summoned Gehazi and said, 'Call the Shunammite woman.' So he called her. When she came to him, he said, 'Take your son.' She came and fell at his feet, bowing to the ground; then she took her son and left" (2 Kings 4:32–37).

The first thing to notice here in this passage is that the healing was not instantaneous.

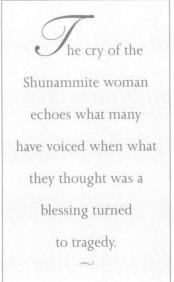

The cry of the Shunammite woman echoes what many have voiced when what they thought was a blessing turned to tragedy.

Healing Through the Power of Prayer

Elisha stretched out on the boy and the boy became warm. Then, after walking back and forth in the room, Elisha tried it again. This time the boy revived.

Some have criticized healing ministries because the healings were not always immediate—as these critics thought they should be to qualify as genuine miracles. But here we see that God cannot be locked into a box. He continually upsets our preconceived notions, as in another

curious healing that Jesus performed: "They came to Bethsaida. Some people brought a blind man to him and begged him to touch him. He took the blind man by the hand and led him out of the village; and when he had put saliva on his eyes and laid his hands on him, he asked him, 'Can you see anything?' And the man looked up and said, 'I can see people, but they look like trees, walking.' Then Jesus laid his hands on his eyes again; and he looked intently and his sight was restored, and he saw everything clearly" (Mark 8:22–25).

The man's healing was not complete until Jesus touched his eyes a second time. The point of this story is not that

> *D*on't give up if after the first attempt you do not achieve the desired results. It is a lesson not just for our prayers for healing but for all of life.

Jesus' healing powers were somehow defective. As we have just seen in the story of the boy at Nain, Jesus performed even greater miracles without hesitation. Rather, it seems he is trying to teach us something here: Don't give up if after the first attempt you do not achieve the desired results. It is a lesson not just for our prayers for healing but for all of life.

This brings up a question that most of us have wondered about at one time or another: How much or how often should we pray about a particular request? What does the biblical injunction "pray without ceasing" (1 Thessalonians 5:17) mean? A nagging thought may enter our heads—that we might be "bothering" God with our repeated and insistent calls to him for healing.

Jesus answered this question himself one day when his disciples asked him to teach them

how to pray. As at many other times, his answer took the form of a parable: "Suppose one of you has a friend, and you go to him at midnight and say to him, 'Friend, lend me three loaves of bread; for a friend of mine has arrived, and I have nothing to set before him.' And he answers from within, 'Do not bother me; the door has already been locked, and my children are with me in bed; I cannot get up and give you anything.' I tell you, even though he will not get up and give him anything because he is his friend, at least because of his persistence he will get up and give him whatever he needs. 'So I say to you, Ask, and it will be given you; search, and you will find; knock, and the door will be opened for you. For everyone who asks

Healing Through the Power of Prayer

receives, and everyone who searches finds, and for everyone who knocks, the door will be opened" (Luke 11:5–10).

Don't give up if your prayers for healing aren't answered on the first attempt! At the same time, we must not mistake the intent of this parable. Jesus is not teaching us here that we can manipulate God into giving us what we want—especially if we are asking for something that would ultimately be harmful to us.

This is made clear by Jesus as he continues: "Is there anyone among you who, if your child asks for a fish, will give a snake instead of a fish? Or if the child asks for an egg, will give a scorpion? If you then, who are evil, know how to give good gifts to your children, how much more will the heavenly Father give the Holy Spirit to those who ask him!" (verses 11–13).

Snakes and scorpions invoke unpleasant thoughts for most of us, though not generally from personal experience. The land of Palestine, however, abounds with these dangerous creatures. In Jesus' day, when people walked over rocky trails wearing sandals, such creatures posed a very real danger.

In this passage, Jesus is saying that there are times when we think we are asking for something good but which could actually cause us harm. He uses the example of the relationship between a child and his parents because it is something each of us can understand, and also because it mirrors our relationship with our heavenly Father.

A child may think that ingesting the entire contents of a bottle of a cherry-flavored medicine would be an excellent idea. But mother and father know better and will refuse the child's pleadings for his own good. In the same way, our heavenly Father knows what truly are the "good gifts" that will enrich our lives. This is a hard teaching to accept, for it sometimes involves measured doses of harsh medicine that are necessary to bring about some greater good.

But we should not be dissuaded from asking, for in this our heavenly Father delights. On one occasion, Jesus admonishes his disciples for trying to keep children away from him: "People were bringing little children to him in order that he might touch them; and the disciples spoke sternly to them. But when Jesus saw this, he was indignant and said to them, 'Let the little children come to me; do not stop them; for it is to such as these that the kingdom of God belongs. Truly I tell you, whoever does not receive the kingdom of God as a little child will never enter it.' And he took them up in his arms, laid his hands on them, and blessed them" (Mark 10:13–16).

We have already seen how Jesus came to defeat the powers

> *Our heavenly Father knows what truly are the "good gifts" that will enrich our lives. This is a hard teaching to accept, for it sometimes involves measured doses of harsh medicine that are necessary to bring about some greater good.*

of darkness and to establish his kingdom. And here we read that it is necessary to become like a little child in order to enter God's kingdom. What does this mean? Jesus is saying that we need to have an attitude of childlike dependence upon God in all things.

Childlike dependence? Grown adults are being asked to act like children? Not in relationship to other people, of course—but in relationship to God we are all as children.

This means trusting that our heavenly Father—not we ourselves—knows what is best in every situation. It means surrendering to the will of God even if this means complete submission, as Jesus taught us in the garden when he himself prayed: "Father, if you are willing, remove this cup from me; yet, not my will but yours be done" (Luke 22:42).

Jesus is not asking anything of us that he himself was not prepared to do, though his submission to the Father's will did not come without great distress: "In his anguish he prayed more earnestly, and his sweat became

> *I*f healing does not follow immediately after praying or being prayed for, we should not assume that the matter is finished. Keep persevering! There is no biblical evidence that in every case healing must be either all or nothing.

Healing Through the Power of Prayer

like great drops of blood falling down on the ground" (Luke 22:44).

We must also be willing to genuinely preface our prayers with the confession "your will be done," for that will ensure that God's best will be done in our lives. Once we have done that, we can rejoice in the privilege of a child: We can come without hesitation to our Father, expecting that our needs will be met.

We should expect that those needs will be met in ways that are delightfully creative beyond what we could ourselves conceive. And it is not only our *needs* that will be met—we can expect that a goodly number of our *desires* will also be granted. A child receives not only clothing but also toys for Christmas.

When children anticipate some joyous event, such as a holiday or birthday, they may inquire about it continually. Or, conversely, when children are concerned about some problem they do not understand, they will take a likewise approach and ask their mother or father about it repeatedly. In the same way, our heavenly Father understands us and expects us to "bother" him in childlike faith if our prayers are not answered on the first attempt.

MODES OF HEALING

If healing does not follow immediately after praying or being prayed for, we should not assume that the matter is finished. Keep persevering! There is no biblical evidence that in every case healing must be either all or nothing. In fact, instantaneous total healing or no healing at all are not the only options—there are other alternatives. Let's look at some of them.

First, there is the possibility that healing may take more

time and prayer. It is often this way with healing, as Father Benedict Heron writes in his insightful book *Channels of Healing Prayer*: "Most healing in answer to prayer is gradual, whether it is healing of spirit, mind or body. Immediate healings are more rare, especially when the sickness is serious. This means that there is normally need for ongoing prayer for healing. We usually suggest to sick people who come to our healing services or sessions that they should come back for further ministry, perhaps come along regularly for quite a time. If we pray with someone for depression or arthritis and there is some improvement, it is probable that if they return for prayer the following week there will  be a further improvement. Moreover, if they do not seem to have benefited the first time, they may begin to improve on the second or third or tenth visit."[1]

We have already discussed biblical examples that illustrate ongoing prayer. Elisha did not raise the Shunammite woman's son with one quick prayer: It took some time before the healing was complete. Also, Jesus applied his hands to the blind man twice before his sight was fully restored.

Second, instead of total physical restoration, the healing may take the form of preventing further deterioration. This is often the case with those further along the path of life, as Father Heron again writes: "Praying for the healing of parts of the body like eyes, ears, backs and chests in elderly people can be very worthwhile even if there is no actual improvement. Prayer can be used by God to slow down the rate of deterio-

Healing Through the Power of Prayer

ration, to help parts of the body to last out longer."[2]

It may also mean that God's grace is the ability to persevere in the midst of a physical problem that will not be healed. This is the type of healing touch that Paul received as he prayed three times for the removal of his "thorn . . . in the flesh" (2 Corinthians 12:7), which most biblical scholars believe was a physical malady. Note how Paul dealt with not being healed: "But he said to me, 'My grace is sufficient for you, for power is made perfect in weak-

> *But he said to me, "My grace is sufficient for you, for power is made perfect in weakness." So, I will boast all the more gladly of my weaknesses, so that the power of Christ may dwell in me.*
>
> *2 Corinthians 12:9*

ness.' So, I will boast all the more gladly of my weaknesses, so that the power of Christ may dwell in me" (2 Corinthians 12:9).

We have no indication that Paul's thorn in the flesh was ever taken away, or that it became progressively worse until it incapacitated him. And so it is with us: If we do not experience total healing, we can at least be thankful and trust that God is preventing whatever ails us from becoming steadily worse.

Third, we may be granted a temporary reprieve that can add productive years to our lives. As we have seen in the example of King Hezekiah, God does on occasion answer prayers for the extension of one's life, as he granted 15 more years of life to Hezekiah. Father Heron gives the following contemporary example: "I remember Winifred in our prayer group whom the doctor had given three months to live with cancer when she was in her seventies. After prayer most of the cancer disappeared to the amazement of the consultant, and Winifred spent the next six years free from trouble with cancer. It is worth adding that her husband of about the same age received a healing of arthritis in his knee on the first evening they came to our prayer group, which was a big help in enabling him to support his wife."[3]

We rejoice when we hear about those whose illnesses seem to improve after prayer, but then we can be disappointed when we learn that they eventually succumbed to the illnesses. This should not discourage us, for their lives might have been shorter and less productive had they not received healing prayer.

Finally, there is the possibility that most of us would prefer

> The healing that we receive may not be for our physical bodies but for our souls, to prepare us to meet our Maker peacefully and with a good conscience.

not to consider. Nonetheless, it is one that each of us will face eventually and is perhaps the most important of all. That is, the healing that we receive may not be for our physical bodies but for our souls, to prepare us to meet our Maker peacefully and with a good conscience.

As Tom Harpur writes, because of our mortality, all physical healings will, in the end, fail: "Western society often acts as though death is the ultimate insult and imposition, an unpleasantness our hi-tech medicine ought somehow to prevent, we know we all have to die eventually. There will come a time in everyone's life when the proper healing prayer or intervention will fittingly be made in the 'voice' of that ancient Christian prayer: that 'at the last' there may be 'a perfect end.'"[4]

There are those who claim it is self-defeating to attach the condition "your will be done" to our prayers. This, they say, only demonstrates a lack of faith. But to ask for God's will to be done is simply to confess that not we but our Creator is in control of all that happens: "This is not doubt or fatalism masking itself as piety. It's a quiet recognition that in the last analysis we are in the hands of God."[5]

Sometimes God answers prayer by enabling the sick individual to pass away in peace and without pain. Father Heron writes about a woman in her forties who was in the last stages of abdominal cancer. The drugs she was receiving for her pain were no longer effective: "When we prayed for her she felt something like an electric current going through her abdomen, and the pain disappeared on the spot. We were still in the ward when the trolley came round with the

Healing Through the Power of Prayer

pain-killers, and to the surprise of the nurse she declined to take any—and she never needed them again. We wondered for a time whether the cancer was healed, but it was not. She died very peacefully about a month later with no pain at all."[6]

It seems at first glance that the prayers for the woman's healing were ineffectual. But anyone who has spent time in a cancer ward knows what a blessing it was for her to die peacefully and without pain.

What is needed is a balance between the "Jesus will always heal" view and the attitude that we should not bother to pray for healing. This is where the caveat "your will be done" is so vital in our prayers. We should earnestly request physical healing. But we should also add that if that is not in God's plan, then we should be granted God's grace and peace. After all, there will be a time in each of our lives when we must prepare to die and go to heaven.

If we concentrate entirely on physical healing and neglect spiritual preparation, the effects can be devastating. Father Heron relates the following tragic illustration: "I can remember a case in which an Anglican vicar complained bitterly that the faith of a dying

If we are adamant and concentrate entirely on physical healing to the neglect of spiritual preparation, which is more needed, the effects can be devastating.

Healing Through the Power of Prayer

parishioner which he had been carefully nurturing was shattered after some charismatic Christians came and prayed over her for healing, giving the impression that Jesus wanted to heal her physically. She was not healed physically and went through a total crisis of faith."[7]

We should note here that Father Heron is not in the least opposed to the Pentecostal belief of praying for healing. In his own life and ministry, he practices the charismatic gifts of the Spirit. But he is concerned about the insistence that God desires in *every* instance to heal physically. In this particular case, he quite rightly felt that the woman needed to be prepared spiritually for heaven.

CHAPTER 10: The Importance of Faith

> When Jesus heard this he was amazed at him, and turning to the crowd that followed him, he said, "I tell you, not even in Israel have I found such faith."
>
> Luke 7:9

In the Gospel of Luke, we read that once when Jesus was entering Capernaum, he was approached by the elders of the city. The fishing village on the shores of the Sea of Galilee had become his adopted home and was more appreciative of his ministry than Nazareth, where  he grew up. Indeed, hundreds of years after the time of Jesus, Capernaum would still be known for its large population of believers in the prophet from Galilee.

The elders of Capernaum came to Jesus to ask him to heal the deathly ill servant of a Roman officer—or centurion. To our twentieth-century minds this may not seem all that unusual. But given the political tensions of the day, it was indeed an extraordinary request. The Jews hated the

Roman occupiers of their country. That enmity would culminate in two successive and ferocious revolts that would level the country and destroy the Jewish nation.

So why are the Jewish elders coming to Jesus on behalf of a Roman military commander? The answer is given in their own words: "He is worthy of having you do this for him, for he loves our people, and it is he who built our synagogue for us" (Luke 7:4–5).

The visitor to Capernaum today can view an imposing structure of white limestone that stands in the midst of the black basaltic buildings of the ancient town. This synagogue, dated to the fourth century, is built over the original synagogue that Jesus knew and to which the elders were referring.

The adventurous visitor can explore the nearby fields

where, hidden in the overgrowth, lie the partially excavated remains of a Roman military camp. It is here that the grievously ill servant of the centurion lay.

Jesus went with the elders to the camp of the servant: "He was not far from the house, the centurion sent friends to say to him, 'Lord, do not trouble yourself, for I am not worthy to have you come under my roof; therefore I did not presume to come to you. But only speak the word, and let my servant be healed. For I also am a man set under authority, with soldiers under me; and I say to one, "Go," and he goes, and to another, "Come," and he comes, and to my slave, "Do this," and the slave does it.' When Jesus heard this he was amazed at him, and turning to

Healing Through the Power of Prayer

the crowd that followed him, he said, 'I tell you, not even in Israel have I found such faith.' When those who had been sent returned to the house, they found the slave in good health" (Luke 7:6–10).

One need only recall how the Jewish people had been chosen by God from among the nations to imagine how this observation must have stung them. Jesus himself had on another occasion stated: "I was sent only to the lost sheep of the house of Israel" (Matthew 15:24). It was to those "lost sheep" that he sent out his disciples. But now, of all people, the one who above all others is commended for his religious faith is none other than a Gentile!

What then was so special about the centurion's faith? Once again, we are brought back to the necessity of child-like faith—though in this instance we might refer to it as implicit trust. It is an attitude of resting in the knowledge that someone is able to do and will do what you have asked. If someone gives an order to those under his command and then follows them around to see if they carry it out, this shows a lack of trust.

It is vital to have a spirit of implicit trust in God when we approach him with our

> We must fully trust that God, far from being a harsh taskmaster, is supremely kind and loving and has good things in store for us.

Healing Through the Power of Prayer

requests. It is an attitude that says: "I have not the slightest doubt but that you can answer my prayer should it be in your will to do so." This, we would suggest, is the meaning of the much-misunderstood passage in the Book of James: "If any of you is lacking in wisdom, ask God, who gives to all generously and ungrudgingly, and it will be given you. But ask in faith, never doubting, for the one who doubts is like a wave of the sea, driven and tossed by the wind; for the doubter, being double-minded and unstable in every way, must not expect to receive anything from the Lord" (James 1:5–8).

Some take the phrase "ask in faith, never doubting" to mean we must believe that we will get what we want. In other words, we must concentrate until we work up a critical mass of faith—and then our prayers will be answered.

But the text is not talking about believing in some supposed power within ourselves that compels God to grant our request. Rather, it is talking about believing in God—that he is able to bring about that which is best for our lives. A little later in the same passage, James makes reference to this: "Do not be deceived, my beloved. Every generous act of giving, with every perfect gift, is from above, coming down from the Father of lights, with whom there is no variation or shadow due to change" (verses 16–17).

And that brings us back to Jesus' teaching about childlike faith and the implicit trust that the centurion of Capernaum displayed. We must fully trust that God, far from being a harsh taskmaster, is supremely kind and loving and has good things in store for all of us.

HELPING OUR UNBELIEF

When Jesus came down from the mountain after the transfiguration, he saw a large crowd gathered around his disciples who were quarreling with them. The topic of their argument? It was about the disciple's inability to heal a boy possessed by an evil spirit. The boy's father had asked the disciples to drive out the spirit, but they could not. No doubt the disciples were hotly defending their inability to do so.

Jesus had just returned from what was truly a "mountaintop experience" of the first order. And no sooner had he descended than he found himself immersed in the problems of the mundane world.

We can sense his frustration as he responds: "'You faithless generation, how much longer must I be among you? How much longer must I put up with you? Bring him to me.' And they brought the boy to him. When the evil spirit saw him, immediately it convulsed the boy, and he fell on the ground and rolled about, foaming at the mouth. Jesus asked the father, 'How long has this been happening to him?' And he said, 'From childhood. It has often cast him into the fire and into the water, to destroy him; but if you are able to do anything, have pity on us and help

> *O*ur heavenly Father knows well that it is when problems have us feeling down and depressed that we need his help the most.

Healing Through the Power of Prayer

us.' Jesus said to him, 'If you are able!—All things can be done for the one who believes.' Immediately the father of the child cried out, 'I believe; help my unbelief!'" (Mark 9:19–24).

All too often this cry of the boy's father resonates within us. There are times when we do not feel that our prayers are accomplishing anything. We want to have faith in God but cannot seem to muster what we think should be the appropriate emotions. But once again we need to remind ourselves that our emotional state does not determine whether or not God will answer our prayers. As Father Heron emphasizes, "healings are not dependent on our feelings or imaginings. Sometimes when all I am feeling is tiredness, unbelief, unworthiness and the desire to finish the healing session more quickly more healing seems to

happen! Jesus is Lord. And healings take place when and how he wishes, not when we feel great or on form!"[1]

What kind of God would we have if he only answered prayers when we were having a good day and feeling positive? Our heavenly Father knows well that it is when problems have us feeling down and depressed that we need his help the most.

ARTICULATING OUR NEEDS

The story of Bartimaeus has much to say about praying for healing. Blind Bartimaeus was sitting by the roadside begging, when one day Jesus passed through the city of Jericho: "When he heard that it was Jesus of Nazareth, he began to shout out and say, 'Jesus, Son of David, have mercy on me!' Many sternly ordered him to be quiet, but he cried out even

Healing Through the Power of Prayer

more loudly, 'Son of David, have mercy on me!' (Mark 10:47–48).

Bartimaeus' persistence here reminds us of the parable of the man who went to his neighbor at night asking for bread. Both demonstrate that God answers our prayers and that we should not be ashamed to ask for help. Similarly, we are encouraged in the Book of Hebrews to pray with boldness: "Let us therefore approach the throne of grace with boldness, so that we may receive mercy and find grace to help in time of need" (Hebrews 4:16).

Though Jesus, as usual, must have been surrounded by his followers and the curious, the sound of the man's voice reached him: "Jesus stood still  and said, 'Call him here.' And they called the blind man, saying to him,

'Take heart; get up, he is calling you.' So throwing off his cloak, he sprang up and came to Jesus. Then Jesus said to him, 'What do you want me to do for you?' The blind man said to him, 'My teacher, let me see again.' Jesus said to him, 'Go; your faith has made you well.' Immediately he regained his sight and followed him on the way" (Mark 10:49–52).

What do you want me to do for you? We can imagine Jesus' penetrating gaze as he spoke these words. They must have pierced Bartimaeus' soul as they do ours. The question forces us to examine the inner motives of our heart. What do each of us really desire when we ask for healing? Are we fantasizing about selling our healing story to the tabloids for a tidy sum?

Our concept of healing is often skin deep. But God may have in mind for us a holistic healing on a far-deeper level

Healing Through the Power of Prayer

than we imagine, as Kenneth Bakken and Kathleen Hofeller write: "Our wounds must also be fully articulated—the physical, psychological, and spiritual aspects of the problem must be uncovered, explored, and experienced. Articulating is, in a sense, dialogue; we get in touch with, acknowledge and listen to all of who we are, especially that which has been denied, repressed, or forgotten . . . . Articulating can be a difficult, time-consuming process, but it is essential to healing. If our wounds are not fully articulated, we may find ourselves echoing the words of Jeremiah: 'They have treated the wound of my people carelessly, saying, "Peace, peace," when there is no peace' (Jeremiah 8:11)."[2]

One of the reasons people are not healed is that they do not want to experience a holistic healing of body, mind, and soul. In many cases, the physical illness may be masking a deeper problem. In such cases, there is little point in removing the physical symptoms without dealing with the root causes.

Bartimaeus cried out for healing, unmindful of what those around him might have thought. His cry for mercy reminds us of the parable of the

> One of the reasons people are not healed is that they do not want to experience a holistic healing of body, mind, and soul.

Pharisee and the tax collector. The Pharisee's prayer was steeped in pride, showing little need for repentance or spiritual healing: "God, I thank you that I am not like other people: thieves, rogues, adulterers, or even like this tax collector. I fast twice a week; I give a tenth of all my income" (Luke 18:11–12).

Truth be told, a lot of us can identify with the Pharisee. We tend to exhibit the same self-righteous attitude towards those who happen to sin more overtly. And there was scarcely anyone who was less deserving of pity than tax collectors. In Jesus' day, they were among the most despised people of Jewish society. Tax collectors were turncoats who worked for the despised Roman occupiers. They received a percentage of what they collected, and their own profit was limited only by how much they could extort from their fellow Jews. It is nothing short of astonishing that it is not the law-abiding Pharisee but the tax collector that Jesus commends. And why? Because of his attitude of brokenness and humility: "But the tax collector, standing far off, would not even look up to heaven, but was beating his breast and saying, 'God, be merciful to me, a sinner!' I tell you, this man went down to his home justified rather than the other; for all who exalt themselves will be

If God heals us, it will be because of his sovereign will, not because we succeeded in striking a bargain with him.

humbled, but all who humble themselves will be exalted'" (verses 13–14).

Be merciful to me! It was this simple, unaffected prayer that Jesus heard. We as well should not be concerned with flowery language: God wants us to share openly from our heart of hearts, as Father Heron explains: "Our prayers are not going to be answered because of their literary excellence or theological development, but because they come from the heart and are said with faith. When we speak to our own human father or brother we do not feel that we have to bother about using refined English. It should be the same when we pray to our Heavenly Father....Usually the simpler the prayer the better."[3]

There is no need to address God using the "thee" and "thou" of some older Bible translations. Those who adapt this manner of praying may succeed in impressing those around them. Their efforts, however, are unlikely to earn them any special favor with God, who understands our vernacular perfectly well. Prayer for healing must be offered with no preconditions. Attempts to manipulate are not likely to succeed. If God heals us, it will be because of his sovereign will, not because we succeeded in striking a bargain with him.

PRAYING WITH BOLDNESS

Theological students are taught obscure Greek and Latin terms that relate to abstract concepts about what God is like. One of these terms is *immutability*, which means that God's nature does not change. From this, some of us have unfortunately developed a rather static idea of a God who resembles a stern, unbending disciplinarian. There wouldn't be much point in pleading with such a God, especially when we add another theological idea—that of the divine Decree. The doctrine of the Decree of God teaches that, at some point in eternity past, all things relating to creation were predetermined. In short, God planned everything that would occur.

There is a certain logical consistency to this idea. After all, God wouldn't be God if he had no control over what was going on in his universe. But it doesn't appear to leave much room for human initiative—or prayer. Why should we pray about something we want to occur if what will happen has already been determined in ages past? We might as well wait to see the inevitable.

While theologians defend the logical necessity of such doc-trines, the Scriptures present us with glimpses of a more dynamic and far richer complexion to our Creator. One such insight into how God relates to us is found in the Book of 2 Kings, where the prophet Isaiah is sent to critically ill King Hezekiah with bad news: "Thus says the Lord: Set your house in order, for you shall die; you shall not recover" (2 Kings 20:1).

The king turned his face to the wall and prayed, weeping bitterly: "Remember now, O Lord, I implore you, how I have walked before you in faithfulness with a whole heart, and have done what is good in your sight" (verse 3).

There you have it: According to the divine plan, Hezekiah's time was up. End of story? Not quite. At this point the unexpected happens. Before Isaiah leaves the king's court the word of the Lord came to him. The

Lord commands Isaiah: "Turn back, and say to Hezekiah prince of my people, Thus says the Lord, the God of your ancestor David: I have heard your prayer, I have seen your tears; indeed, I will heal you; on the third day you shall go up to the house of the Lord. I will add fifteen years to your life. I will deliver you and this city out of the hand of the king of Assyria" (verses 5–6).

So much for the so-called unalterable, set-in-stone divine plan for every detail of our lives. This passage gives the other side of that plan—the human side. It speaks volumes about God's willingness to listen when we pray to him. While the length of our lifespan is determined by God—there appears to be some flexibility in how he arrives at the limit of our years.

This balance between the divine plan and human initiative is nearly impossible to grasp. It seems inherently contradictory, but in reality it is a profound aspect of the nature of God that is simply beyond human comprehension. As Saint Ignatius of Loyola put it in another context—that of salvation: we should pray as though everything depends on God, and work as though everything depends upon us.

That might not satisfy the logicians, but it fairly represents the breadth of biblical evidence about the divine and human roles in determining events. So

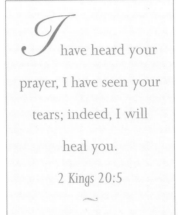

I have heard your prayer, I have seen your tears; indeed, I will heal you.

2 Kings 20:5

while we pray for healing, we also have a responsibility to do what we can to avoid sickness and preserve our health. There is no excuse for abusing our bodies: We have already seen that they are the temple of God.

But we should not go to the other extreme and overemphasize human responsibility. The mistaken belief that the whole of the burden is on our shoulders can lead to anxiety. Our ability to influence events is ultimately limited. After all, despite our best efforts, there will come a day when our mortal bodies will fail. As Jesus himself says: "And can any of you by

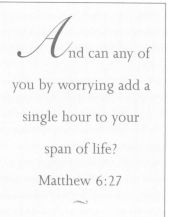

And can any of you by worrying add a single hour to your span of life?

Matthew 6:27

worrying add a single hour to your span of life?" (Matthew 6:27). While worrying cannot extend our lifespan, the example of Hezekiah gives us hope that prayer can.

It sometimes seems to take a long time to get a divine response to our prayers—as if they are laboriously processed by some heavenly bureaucracy and answered when they make their way to the top of the list. But in this passage, we see an immediate response to Hezekiah's prayer that beats even e-mail. Before Isaiah leaves the king's palace, he is sent back with the answer. And in our lives also, more often than we are aware, the divine response is just as swift—some-

Healing Through the Power of Prayer

times it just takes awhile for the answer to be delivered to us.

And what an answer it is! Hezekiah is granted 15 more years to his life—another confirmation that God is ultimately in control of our times and seasons. And he can also change the course of events around us: Hezekiah is promised that the city of Jerusalem would not fall to the dreaded Assyrians, a fact confirmed by the annals of history.

There is one final question: What would have been the outcome if Hezekiah had not brought his petition before his Maker? Very likely, he would have died according to Isaiah's original prophecy.

This passage gives us a unique insight into the nature of our interaction with the Divine. While there is a plan for our lives, there are times when

that plan is subject to change. It is a mistake to picture God as an easygoing, forgetful grandfather who can be cajoled into giving us what we want. Perhaps one of the hardest lessons for us to learn is that God cannot be manipulated. But on the other hand, when we pray, God does listen and he can alter the course of events.

With Hezekiah that meant physical healing—as it can also be for us. And when God does heal, we must be prepared for the unexpected, for God's ways of healing are truly inscrutable. God will not be limited to our formulations: His means of healing are wonderful beyond knowing and infinite in variety. Every case is unique, just as every person is unique.

CHAPTER 11:
Miracle Workers

> But God chose what is foolish in
> the world to shame the wise; God
> chose what is weak in the world to
> shame the strong.
>
> 1 Corinthians 1:27

If the experiences we have already seen are any indication, it seems safe to conclude that God delights in using unexpected means and unusual people to bring healing. Solanus Casey was one of the latter. Solanus was one of the most effective miracle workers of our century even though he had no television ministry, held  no healing crusades, and wrote no best-selling books. He held the same unassuming job for 40 years and accumulated no material possessions. By human standards—judged by his early failures—he was destined for an inconsequential career. But out of the ashes of his failure rose a remarkable ministry. This is the story of an extraordinary yet unpretentious person.

Solanus Casey was born in 1870 into a large Midwestern family. As he sought to find his way in life, he tried a succession of jobs. He finally settled on the vocation of streetcar conductor. It led to a profound spiritual crisis that would alter the course of his life.

Casey's streetcar route took him through a rough part of town, and he kept his eyes open for trouble. One afternoon, he came upon a crowd gathered on the tracks ahead. He stopped the streetcar and got out, pushing his way through the crowd.

There he saw a violent scene that was the object of the crowd's morbid curiosity: A drunken sailor had raped and stabbed a young woman. The sailor was standing over her, cursing as he staggered in his intoxicated delirium.

The incident affected Casey deeply. Though not particularly religious, he felt moved to pray for the girl and the sailor. As time went on, he found his faith increasing. He had a growing desire to pray for and

serve others. He decided the best way to accomplish his goal

would be to become a priest.

Casey enrolled in the seminary of the diocese of Milwaukee, Wisconsin, but soon found himself struggling with the rigors of academic life. To add to his difficulties, most of his professors taught in German, of which he understood little.

In 1895, the 25-year-old Casey was dismissed from the seminary. As a consolation, his advisors recommended he enter a religious order as a laybrother. But this would have been a step down from his original goal of becoming a priest, and Casey was not ready to give up his dream.

Fortunately, the Catholic church has many orders to choose from. The next year, Casey entered the Capuchin

Healing Through the Power of Prayer

order, and in 1897, he completed his novitiate at Saint Bonaventure Monastery in Detroit, Michigan.

Casey then found himself back in Milwaukee, this time studying at the Capuchin seminary. Once again the native language of the city's large immigrant population threatened his success. As before, his classes were taught in German, which he had managed to learn only imperfectly.

After seven years, Solanus was scheduled to graduate. Due to his poor grades, his professors were reluctant to grant his ordination. But this time Casey found a champion in the elderly director of the seminary, Father Anthony, who stated prophetically: "We shall ordain Father Solanus, and as a priest he will be to the people something like the Cure of Ars."[1] The director was referring to Saint John Vianney, the Cure of Ars, who, like Casey, was a poor student who became a great wonder-worker.

In the end, the seminary granted Casey a limited ordination. He became a simplex priest, which meant he could not formally preach or administer the sacrament of penance. He would also not be permitted to wear the distinctive hood that was the trademark of the Capuchin order.

After years of preparation for the priesthood, many others would have considered this a humiliating defeat. But not Solanus: He gracefully accepted the limitations that had been placed upon him.

At the outset, there was little to indicate that Father Solanus Casey would distinguish himself in his religious work. He spent the next 40 years of his career in the lowly position of a porter, greeting visitors to the monasteries in New York

Healing Through the Power of Prayer

City, where he served. But just as Moses spent 40 years of preparation in the wilderness before leading the Israelites, God used Casey's long years to develop a powerful ministry of healing.

Working as a doorkeeper put Casey in contact with those who came to the monastery; they found him to be blessed with an unusual measure of humility and patience. He listened to their problems and offered wise advice. As time went on, more and more people started coming to the monastery just to see Father Casey.

As his reputation spread, Casey was given the responsibility of promoting the intercessory prayer ministry of the Capuchin order, called the Seraphic Mass Association. The name came from Saint Francis of Assisi, who, according to church tradition, had a vision of a high-ranking class of angels, called seraphim. Around the world, Capuchins pray for needs expressed to the association. Bert Ghezzi, in his book *Miracles of the Saints*, describes what happened: "Shortly after Solanus started signing people up, extraordinary things began to happen. Reports of spiritual and physical healings streamed in. People were being healed of all sorts

> *But just as Moses spent 40 years of preparation in the wilderness before leading the Israelities, God used Casey's long years to develop a powerful ministry of healing.*

Healing Through the Power of Prayer

of ailments—pneumonia, heart disease, memory loss, insanity, lameness, cataracts, polio, alcoholism, gangrene, and blindness, to name just a few."[2]

As word of Father Casey's healing powers spread, he was permitted by his superiors to begin leading a weekly healing service. At the service, an increasing number of sick and infirmed were ministered to. Over the next two decades, records showed that literally thousands of people received healing.

One of these was an eight-month-old infant named Raymond, who was suffering from mastoiditis in both ears. One evening, the fevered child was brought to the hospital. In those days, before the discovery of antibiotics, doctors had few tools with which to cure the potentially fatal condition. One of these involved an experimental and delicate operation on the inner ear.

The procedure was planned for the next morning. Raymond's mother was beside herself with fear. She knew that the surgery, which involved drilling holes to relieve pressure on the inner ears, was fraught with danger. She could not bear the thought of her son being subjected to an operation with dubious chances for success.

When she and her son were left alone together in the room, she took action. She bundled

*O*ver the next two decades, records showed that literally thousands of people received healing.

up her weakened son and spirited him out of the hospital to where her brother, notified in advance, was waiting in a car. Driving on their way back home, the confused mother scarcely knew what to do. She did not want her son undergoing the operation—but what other option did she have?

Then she remembered hearing about Father Casey and his remarkable powers of healing. She decided to give him a try and told her brother to drive to the monastery. She was greatly relieved to see that Casey was at his post at the door. He reached for the infant as the child's mother poured out her story. "Please help him!" she cried.

Casey asked the child's name and prayed a simple prayer for his healing. He encouraged Raymond's mother to have faith in God and in his unfailing promises. Casey left her with the assurance: "He will be better by morning—and don't worry. He won't need an operation."[3]

With her hopes lifted, the mother returned home with her son. But would Raymond be healed as Father Casey promised? During the night, the child's nightclothes were drenched in sweat as his fever continued unabated. His anxious mother was beginning to wonder if she had made a foolish decision by taking her child from the hospital to have the doorkeeper at a monastery pray for him.

Finally, she fell asleep. When she awoke, it was morning. She rushed to Raymond's bed and was alarmed to find him still and cool to the touch. But bending over him, she rejoiced to feel his soft breath against her cheek. The fever was past.

The grateful parents returned to the monastery and showed a now recovered Raymond to

Healing Through the Power of Prayer

Father Casey, who shared their joy but not their astonishment. He had seen God work similar miracles countless times through the years. The next day, Raymond was examined by the doctors and pronounced healthy. No operation was necessary, and the boy returned home with his happy parents.

God uses unexpected vessels, such as Father Casey, to show us that he is the one who is really performing the miracle. It is not necessary to attend a healing crusade featuring a prominent personality to experience a miracle, although there are certainly times when God uses such means as well. But just as often, he will choose to use someone of modest stature.

It surely was a humbling experience for many to approach the lowly gatekeeper of a monastery for healing. This reminds us of another story from biblical times, that of Naaman, the commander of the army of the king of Aram—what is now Syria. Naaman was a man of immense stature. In a time and culture that prided itself above all in military power, he had attained the pinnacle of achievement: "Naaman, commander of the army of the king of Aram, was a great man and in high favor with his master, because by

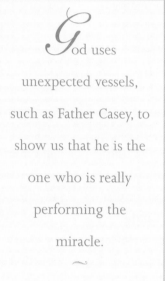

God uses unexpected vessels, such as Father Casey, to show us that he is the one who is really performing the miracle.

Healing Through the Power of Prayer

him the Lord had given victory to Aram. The man, though a mighty warrior, suffered from leprosy" (2 Kings 5:1).

Leprosy. The word alone conveyed a stark terror in the ancient world. Those afflicted with the dreaded disease were often banished from their town or village, doomed to spend their days in isolation from the rest of society. They were unable to hold gainful employment and were reduced to begging.

To warn others, they were required to announce their presence by crying out "unclean" to all who approached. This was the fate that awaited proud Naaman when he discovered he had a telltale whitened patch of skin that signaled leprosy. In one fell swoop, the proud Syrian commander was destined to fall from his lofty position to that of a beggar.

As if the fact of having leprosy were not enough, God was not through with humbling Naaman. Evidently there were no miracle workers in Syria, so Naaman was compelled to follow the advice of—of all people—his servant girl. The girl, a captive Jewess, had urged him to seek healing at the hands of a prophet from Israel—the age-old enemy of Syria. Taking along his customary retinue, Naaman went to see Elisha: "So Naaman came with his horses and chariots, and halted at the entrance of Elisha's house. Elisha sent a messenger to him, saying, 'Go, wash in the Jordan seven times, and your flesh shall be restored and you shall be clean.' But Naaman became angry and went away, saying, 'I thought that for me he would surely come out, and stand and call on the name of the Lord his God, and would wave his hand over

Healing Through the Power of Prayer

the spot, and cure the leprosy! Are not Abana and Pharpar, the rivers of Damascus, better than all the waters of Israel? Could I not wash in them, and be clean?' He turned and went away in a rage" (verses 9–12).

Not only did Elisha fail to give his distinguished guest due honor by welcoming him personally, but Naaman considered his instructions insulting. Whatever romantic images the Jordan River may conjure up in one's mind, in reality for much of the year it is little more than a muddy stream. To Naaman, it was far less inviting than the rivers flowing through the well-watered plain of Damascus.

Naaman knew exactly how he wanted to be healed. He  expected Elisha to recognize the eminent personage who had come to him. Then (we can imagine him thinking) it would be nice if the prophet would not take up any more of his time than necessary and simply wave his hand over the leprous spot. When things didn't proceed as he expected, he became angry and stomped away.

How easy it is for us also to try to tell God not only what miracle we want in our lives, but exactly how he should accomplish it. But our Creator has his own purposes, not the least of which is to teach us that he is in control—not us. Fortunately, Naaman was willing to learn this lesson. His servants succeeded in convincing him to give it a try, and he swallowed his pride and followed Elisha's instructions: "So he went down and immersed himself seven times in the Jordan, according to the word of the man of God; his flesh

Healing Through the Power of Prayer

was restored like the flesh of a young boy, and he was clean. Then he returned to the man of God, he and all his company; he came and stood before him and said, 'Now I know that there is no God in all the earth except in Israel'" (verses 14–15).

God could have healed Naaman without having him bathe in the River Jordan. As we have already observed in Jesus' use of clay and spittle, it is doubtful that the means—in this case the waters of the Jordan—had any curative powers. We have no indication that anyone besides Naaman was asked to bathe in it for healing. In the several recorded instances in the gospels where Jesus healed lepers, none of them were asked to wash in the Jordan or any other river.

The point of using such unusual means of healing was to bring Naaman to the point of acknowledging the one true God. And so it is with us. God may bring healing into our lives in a totally inexplicable way—so that we can only conclude: "God must have done it!"

Clay and spittle. Dipping in the Jordan. The healing means that God uses cannot be reduced to a formula. Healing cannot be conjured like a magical incantation, as Father Heron writes: "Praying for healing is not a matter of mastering a technique, of learn-

> *But our Creator has his own purposes, not the least of which is to teach us that he is in control—not us.*

ing precise formulas, of following a set of rules. It is Jesus who heals people not us, and he heals people when and how he wills. So all we can do is to beg him in his infinite mercy to bless people with his healing touch of love. Basically what is required of us is that we try to pray authentically, which means that we seek to pray with faith, hope, love, and humility."[4]

God heals people when and how he wills. There should be no doubt in our minds who is in control: We should not confuse the messenger who delivers the gift from the giver. And just to make sure, our heavenly Father uses the unexpected, like clay, spittle, a muddy river—and Father Solanus Casey.

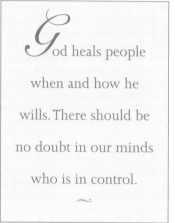

God heals people when and how he wills. There should be no doubt in our minds who is in control.

Although there are no formulas that will guarantee healing, we are not devoid of a procedure to follow. We read in the gospels that the disciples "anointed with oil many who were sick and cured them" (Mark 6:13). The Book of James reiterates the use of anointing oil in healing: "Are any among you sick? They should call for the elders of the church and have them pray over them, anointing them with oil in the name of the Lord. The prayer of faith will save the sick" (James 5:14–15).

Down through the centuries, Christians have anointed the sick with oil as they prayed for healing. Until the ninth century, the rite was used primarily for physical healing. The faithful would often have oil in their homes that had been blessed by a priest or a bishop, which they would use in times of illness.

Beginning with the ninth century, the sacrament of anointing the sick was gradually changed into a rite for the spiritual preparation of the dying, or Extreme Unction. In our own time, there has been a renewed emphasis upon physical healing and restoration. The Second Vatican Council, convened between 1962 and 1965, recognized that the use of oil for healing is not just for those on their deathbeds.

Accordingly, the Council changed the name of the sacrament to the Sacrament of the Anointing of the Sick. We read in one official church document of the era: "Part of the plan laid out by God's provi-dence is that we should fight strenuously against all sickness and carefully seek the blessings of good health, so that we may fulfill our role in human society and in the Church . . . the faithful should be educated to ask for the sacrament of anointing and, as soon as the right time comes, to receive it with full faith and they should not follow the wrongful practice of delaying the reception of the sacrament. All who care for the sick should be taught the meaning and purpose of the sacrament."[5]

The sacrament is also to be used with those suffering from emotional maladies. The document continues to state: "Those who are judged to have a serious mental illness and who would be strengthened by the sacrament may be anointed."[6]

There is a beautiful prayer that is offered by the priest as he blesses the oil:

"God of all consolation,
you chose and sent your Son to
   heal the world.
Graciously listen to our prayer
   of faith:
send the power of your Holy
   Spirit, the Consoler,
into this precious oil, this
   soothing ointment,
this rich gift, this fruit of the
   earth.
Bless this oil and sanctify it for
   our use.
Make this oil a remedy for all
   who are anointed with it;
heal them in body, in soul, and
   in spirit,
and deliver them from every
   affliction.
We ask this through our Lord
   Jesus Christ, your Son,
who lives and reigns with you
   and the Holy Spirit,
one God, for ever and ever."[7]

Skeptics may ask: What is so
special about oil that has been
blessed by a priest? We have
already seen, for example, in
Jesus' miracle of the clay and
spittle, that the material used
had little or no curative powers.
There is no difference in the
chemical composition of blessed
oil and nonblessed oil. So why
should we not use ordinary oil
from our own kitchens?

The reason for blessing the
oil goes back to the Book of
James, where the sick are not
told to anoint themselves with
any oil that might be available.
Rather, they should "call for the
elders of the church and have
them pray over them, anointing
them with oil in the name of
the Lord."

In calling upon the leaders
of the Church to anoint us, we
are making a public request
for healing. By doing so, we
realize that we cannot attempt
to live our lives in isolation.
We need help from others,
and, in this case especially,
from those who have been
gifted in the healing arts.

The practice of keeping a bottle of blessed oil in one's home reflected this principle. Even if the priest was unable to come to apply the oil himself, by using consecrated oil the faithful were recognizing those who had been vested with ecclesiastical authority.

There are some Christians who would adamantly deny any such thing as a blessed substance—whether oil or any other physical material. However, these skeptics should consider what happened to Jesus: "And wherever he went, into villages or cities or farms, they laid the sick in the marketplaces, and begged him that they might touch even a fringe of his cloak; and all who touched it were healed" (Mark 6:56).

Even the touching of Jesus' clothing brought healing to those who gathered around him. "That was Jesus," some may protest, "not mere mortals like us." But the healing power of divinely touched materials has not been limited to Jesus. We have already seen what happened in the Book of Acts: "God did extraordinary miracles through Paul, so that when handkerchiefs or aprons that had touched his skin were brought to the sick, their dis-

> *I*n calling upon the leaders of the Church to anoint us, we are making a public request for healing. By doing so, we realize that we cannot attempt to live our lives in isolation.

eases left them, and the evil spirits came out of them" (19:11–12).

Verses like these can threaten the theology of those who deny the power of healing. But denominational prejudices should not be permitted to blind us to the possibility that God may use a physical means to bring healing. We should avail ourselves freely of the anointing of oil by our spiritual leaders—and not just once, as the official Catholic church teaching after Vatican II counsels: "The sacrament may be repeated if the sick person recovers after being anointed and then again falls ill or if during the same illness the person's condition becomes more serious."[8]

This also gives us a clue as to how often we should pray for healing. As with the anointing with oil, the answer seems to be: We should not become discouraged, but pray for healing as long as the need continues.

LAYING HANDS ON THE SICK

Along with the anointing of oil, the laying on of hands is another biblical means that God uses to heal. Jesus often touched those who came to him for healing: "As the sun was setting, all those who had

> God did extraordinary miracles through Paul, so that when handkerchiefs or aprons that had touched his skin were brought to the sick, their diseases left them.
>
> Acts 19:11–2

any who were sick with various kinds of diseases brought them to him; and he laid his hands on each of them and cured them" (Luke 4:40). He also used touch as a means of blessing, as when the children were brought to him: "And he laid his hands on them and went on his way" (Matthew 19:15).

Jesus promised that his followers would perform miracles by the laying on of hands: "They will lay their hands on the sick, and they will recover" (Mark 16:18). Thus we find the Apostle Paul laying his hands upon the father of Publius: "Paul visited him and cured him by praying and putting his hands on him" (Acts 28:8).

How fitting it is that the laying on of hands was used by the apostles to heal people, for it is a natural human response to sickness and injury. How many of us can remember our mother's cool hand on our

fevered brow as we lay in our sick bed—and how comforting it was?

Human touch can be an expression of sympathy, to be sure, but more than that: It seems to convey beneficial effects—real or imagined. This is what the child senses as they trot off after having their mother gently lay gentle hands on their bumps and bruises.

That there is indeed healing power in both the anointing with oil and the laying of hands is shown by the remarkable testimony of Dr. M. Jessudas. After losing weight and experiencing weakness in his legs and breathing difficulties, Dr. Jessudas was admitted to the intensive care unit of a hospital. He was diagnosed with a malignant tumor of the spine. Dr. Jessudas relates the shock of learning that he had cancer: "Being a family man with two young children, my first reaction was one of panic. I had never experienced such an emotional crisis. However, being a medical man I had faith in medical science. But, notwithstanding my hopes, I continued to deteriorate even after radiation treatment. As no further treatment was available, after radiation I was sent home and the doctors had given up hope. I lay in the bed paralyzed from the waist down and partially paralyzed in the arms."[9]

In crises like these, where does one turn? While having a belief in a higher power, by his own admission, Dr. Jessudas did not think much of the healing potential of prayer. But that all changed when a fellow doctor introduced him to a charismatic prayer group.

Several members of the group came to his home to pray for him. Then they anointed him with oil and laid hands on him for healing. As they did, he felt a warm sensation in his spine and legs.

Such physical sensations are often reported, but once again we cannot reduce the healing process to a formula. Father Heron notes the different physical reactions people have as they are being prayed for: "I

> *While having a belief in a higher power, by his own admission, Dr. Jessudas did not think much of the healing potential of prayer. But that all changed.*

also normally ask someone I am praying with whether they feel anything. They quite often say that they are feeling peaceful, perhaps very peaceful. They may also say that they feel they are experiencing warmth or heat going through their whole body or through the part of the body which is being prayed over. They also sometimes talk of tingling or glowing sensations or an electric-like force going through them. Occasionally they say they are feeling cold or that a part of their body feels cold. They often say that they feel nothing. They may very occasionally even say they feel worse!"[10]

Dr. Jessudas noticed, to his amazement, an immediate improvement in his mobility. In subsequent prayers and anointings with oil, his condition steadily improved until he was

completely healed. "From being totally bedridden I am now free from cancer and able to walk with little difficulty and look after my family. Without the Charismatic Renewal and the group's prayers, I am quite certain that this new chapter in my life would not have taken place. The group prayed over me frequently for six months. The tumor in my back got smaller and smaller until it disappeared and my mobility increased. I am now working full-time as a hospital consultant again."[11]

Along with his physical healing, he experienced spiritual renewal.

And so the transformation of Dr. Jessudas' body, soul, and spirit was complete.

Healing Through the Power of Prayer

CHAPTER 12:
Healing Places

Jesus said to him, "Stand up, take
your mat and walk." At once the
man was made well, and he took up
his mat and began to walk.

John 5:8–9

Are there special places where one can go to experience a miracle? We have already seen on the pages of Scripture how specially anointed individuals had the ability to perform healings. Along with Jesus, the prophet Elisha, the apostles, and others were gifted. We have also examined how physical objects and substances, such as handkerchiefs and conse-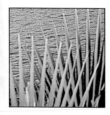crated oil, can be used to convey healing powers.

But what about healing places? Here the biblical evidence is scant—unless we consider the controversial example of the Pool of Bethesda. As already explained, the pool was the site of a healing shrine dedicated to the Greco-Roman god Aesculapius. So we know that the pagan Gentiles of Jesus' time—and doubtlessly quite a few Jews—considered the place to have healing powers. But does the Bible say that the Pool of Bethesda was actually a place where people went to be healed?

The answer to that depends on which translation of the bible you use. All translations include the following description: "Now in Jerusalem by the Sheep Gate there is a pool, called in Hebrew Bethzatha, which has five porticoes. In these lay many invalids—blind, lame, and paralyzed" (John 5:2–3).

However, and here is where the controversy begins, some ancient manuscripts of the Bible include the following verse: "For an angel of the Lord went down at certain seasons into the pool, and stirred up the water; whoever stepped in first after the stirring of the water was made well from whatever disease that person had" (verse 4).

This could be considered evidence of such a healing place—a particular location where divine miracles were known to take place. However, because some ancient manuscripts include this verse while others do not, scholars are of differing minds as to whether or not it belongs in the sacred text. Accordingly, some modern translations of the Bible include this verse, while others do not.

But it is noteworthy that a few verses later, in undisputed text, there is a reference to the stirring of the waters. We read that the invalid complains, "I have no one to put me into the pool when the water is stirred up; and while I am making my way, someone else steps down ahead of me" (verse 7).

There seems little doubt that the Pool of Bethesda was considered a place of healing, for the text itself says that a "great number of disabled people" went there in hope of a cure.

But do such healing places exist today? The Roman

Healing Through the Power of Prayer

Catholic church, for one, believes the answer to that question is yes. Millions of faithful Catholics make pilgrimages in hope of healing, to places that include Chartres Cathedral and Lourdes in France, among others.

A METHODIST AT LOURDES

Vera Norris, a lifelong Methodist who lived in England, suffered for decades from rheumatoid arthritis and osteoarthritis. She was told by her doctors that she would never walk again. To complicate matters, the maculae of her eyes had been damaged by drugs she had taken for her condition. In 1969, she was declared partially blind. Her eyes continued to deteriorate until, in 1984, she was registered as blind.

Norris was in the depths of despair and angry with God

because of the loss of her sight and having to endure constant pain from her arthritis. Then, she was introduced to a prayer group that proved to be a spiritual encouragement to her. Vera had heard about the Rosary Basilica at Lourdes where people were reported to be healed. In 1986, Norris decided to join several members of her prayer group on a pilgrimage to the healing shrine.

The famous town of Lourdes of the Gave de Pau River in southwest France gained fame in 1858, when a 14-year-old girl named Bernadette Subirous reported a series of visions of the Virgin Mary. The visions occurred at the grotto of Massabielle, near the river. On one occasion, she was directed to dig for a spring in the grotto. To her surprise, as she dug, water came forth. Today, the spring flows at a rate of 32,000 gallons a day.

Miraculous cures began to be reported at Lourdes, and after examining the evidence for healings closely, the Catholic church awarded official sanction to Lourdes as a place of pilgrimage. In time, a basilica and other facilities were built to accommodate the millions of pilgrims who made their way to the site.

Thousands of healings have been reported at Lourdes, so many that an organization called The International Medical Commission was established in Paris to examine the merits of the cures. The commission has dismissed a large number whose veracity could not be established or which could be attributed to spontaneous remission. As of 1984, 64 cases have been officially designated as miracles.

One of the more well-documented healings in recent times is told in the book *The Extraordinary Cure of Vittorio Michelli.* Michelli had a large cancerous tumor in his left hip, which had disintegrated the bone to the extent that his upper leg bone was left completely unattached. After his doctors had given him no hope of a cure, he went on a pilgrimage to Lourdes, where he bathed in the curative springs. As he did, he felt a warmth spreading throughout his body.

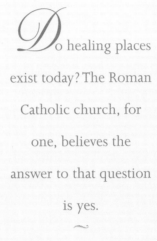

*D*o healing places exist today? The Roman Catholic church, for one, believes the answer to that question is yes.

Healing Through the Power of Prayer

He bathed several more times in the waters and reported feeling much improved. Returning home, he continued to improve and, suspecting that healing had taken place in his hip, he went to his doctors for an examination. When the X rays came back, the doctors discovered that the tumor had shrunk. While tumor shrinkage is often accomplished with radiation and chemotherapy, it rarely occurs spontaneously.

Michelli's doctors carefully documented his progress over the next several months. They were astounded to discover that not only had the tumor disappeared, but the hip bone had regenerated, something deemed impossible by medical science.

Despite documented miracles like that of Vittorio Michelli, Lourdes is not without its critics. Skeptic Joe Nickell, in his book Looking for a Miracle, considers Lourdes to be a fraud. He builds his case on a number of spurious "healings" that supposedly took place at the shrine: "Some of the cases of attempted healings at Lourdes are heart-rending. Such a case was that of a seven-year-old boy from St. Joseph, Michigan, named Randy Eckman. In 1956 his neighbors raised the money to permit his mother, a Lutheran, to take Randy to Lourdes to cure his leukemia since doctors had given the child only a year to live. The *Chicago Sun-Times* featured a series of articles on the pilgrimage. Afterwards, Randy's mother claimed her son had made a 100-percent improvement. He even returned to school, whereupon the *Sun-Times* headlined 'Randy Romps His Age after Shrine Trip.' With tragic irony, however, on February 5, 1957, exactly one year after the little boy had departed for Lourdes, he was baptized as a Catholic and died. The *Sun-Times* placed the story on an inside page."[1]

It is heartbreaking to see the desperate hopes of parents for the healing of their child being cruelly dashed. Nickell argues that unfortunate illustrations like Randy Eckman prove definitively that no miracles are occurring at Lourdes.

But cases like that of Randy Eckman, tragic though they are, do not disprove all the reported healings at Lourdes. In fact, it should come as no surprise that many—even the vast majority—of those who go to Lourdes come away with little or no discernible improvement. We have already seen that, for reasons unknown to us, God does not always answer our prayers for healing as we want him to. It may be the case that the healing is gradual rather than instantaneous and thus not apparent until some time after visiting Lourdes. And it may be that the healing that God intends is spiritual rather than physical.

The fact that by 1984 only 64 reported cases had been declared miracles does not discredit Lourdes. If anything, the low number attests to the strict standards of examination on the part of the International Medical Commission. It should be noted that there may well have been additional genuine miracles among the thousands of others that the commission has examined.

> *And it may be that the healing that God intends is spiritual rather than physical.*

Healing Through the Power of Prayer

However, because they were not able to obtain the proper documentation necessary to validate them, they could not be declared miracles. In addition, for whatever reasons, many other testimonies are not brought to the attention of the committee.

There must be some reason why the healing shrine of Lourdes, which continues to attract some two million faithful pilgrims each year, is one of the most popular pilgrimages in Western Christendom. The reason—which attracts even non-Catholics like

Vera Norris—is the hope that the healing that others have experienced will happen also to them.

This was Norris's prayer as she journeyed to Lourdes. Since she could not walk unaided and was legally blind, she was confined to a wheelchair. Norris asked God to touch her, and her prayers were answered—beginning with the spiritual renewal of her soul: "One morning, during the Healing Mass in the new hospital chapel in Lourdes, I began to weep copiously. I wept for a long time and I felt that all that was sinful in me had been washed away. My heart was filled with joy. Later on in the day, another pilgrim prophesied to me that what I had just experienced was only the beginning. After

> *Norris was able to kneel down and pray. Since that time, much of her vision has been restored.*

Healing Through the Power of Prayer

lunch we went on a walking tour of Lourdes, but I sat in the wheelchair."[2]

Later, as the members of her group formed a prayer circle to intercede for healing, Norris again felt the hand of the Divine upon her: "Suddenly, I felt a sensation of being lifted up into the air in my chair and this happened three times. I heard a clear voice saying: 'Get up and walk.' But I had not walked unaided for twenty-three years and I was nervous. The voice ordered: 'Ask Joe.' I looked around and I saw Joe (Penfold) in a shaft of sunlight, some distance away. Normally, I would not have been able to see him. At my request Joe came over and helped me to rise from the chair. I stood up, turned round and started to walk slowly and effortlessly. The miracle had happened."[3]

For the first time in more than two decades, Norris was

able to kneel down and pray. Since that time, much of her vision has been restored.

Norris underwent an inward, spiritual healing before her body experienced a considerable degree of physical restoration. Her testimony reminds us once again of the relationship between the body, soul, and spirit.

Kelsey writes: "There is no sharp line of demarcation between the religious, spiritual, emotional, and physical— between the body and the psyche. If it can be shown that religious life has a vital effect upon the total emotional life of human beings, upon that which Christians are apt to call the soul, then it may be assumed that it can have a like effect upon the body of the believer."[4]

Healing Through the Power of Prayer

Part IV:

When Healing Doesn't Come

But where shall wisdom be found?
And where is the place of understanding?
Mortals do not know the way to it, and it is
not found in the land of the living. It is
hidden from the eyes of all living, and
concealed from the birds of the air. God
understands the way to it, and he knows its
place. For he looks to the ends of the
earth, and sees everthing under the
heavens.

Job 28:12-13, 21, 23-24

CHAPTER 13: The Power of Forgiveness

> Why have you struck us down so
> that there is no healing for us?
> We look for peace, but find no
> good; for a time of healing, but
> there is terror instead.
>
> Jeremiah 14:19

Tom Harpur tells a story about a woman who went to see a physician, Dr. Alfred Price, who, as a part of his medical practice, believes in the laying on of hands for healing. The woman was suffering from a painful arthritic condition that conventional medicine was  unable to relieve, and she wanted to try the laying on of hands.

Dr. Price, aware of the connection between body, soul, and spirit, makes a point of questioning his patients about their emotional and spiritual condition. As part of his examination, he asked the woman about her emotional state and goals for her life. Her responses raised no suspicions until he brought up the subject of her family.

At this, the woman's whole demeanor changed. The one

great thorn in her side, she confessed, was none other than her daughter-in-law. With bitterness she described that her son's wife had succeeded not only in ruining his life but hers as well. She droned on and on with a long catalog of what she viewed as the unfortunate woman's failures. Finally, when the doctor was able to get a word in edgewise, he tried to explain to her that holding grudges can be a barrier to healing: "Look, I'm not saying all arthritis is caused by anger and frustration," he told her, "but I don't think you'll ever get relief until you go to your daughter-in-law and make up your quarrel."

With that, the woman jumped up and huffed out of the room, calling out behind her: "The arthritis hurts, but it doesn't hurt enough for that!"[1]

It is bad enough to be hurting without being told by

some well-meaning counselor that illness is the result of spiritual problems. The Scriptures tell us that we are not to assess blame: "Let us therefore no longer pass judgment on one another, but resolve instead never to put a stumbling block or hindrance in the way of another" (Romans 14:13). When we speak about hindrances to healing, it must be done in a spirit of encouragement—not condemnation.

THE UNFORGIVING SPIRIT

The woman in Dr. Price's office found it impossible to forgive her daughter-in-law for her faults, whether real or imaginary. No more compelling words regarding forgiveness have been spoken than those uttered by Jesus on the cross:

Healing Through the Power of Prayer

"When they came to the place that is called The Skull, they crucified Jesus there with the criminals, one on his right and one on his left. Then Jesus said, 'Father, forgive them; for they do not know what they are doing'" (Luke 23:33–34).

These words of Jesus' were not spoken during a time of comfortable reflection, but in the midst of suffering. The Romans used crucifixion as a particularly brutal means of instilling fear into a rebellious population. For that reason, crucifixions were public events. The unclothed condemned lay exposed to all who passed by.

Crucifixion involved an excruciatingly slow asphyxiation combined with the torment of having to push up for breath against legs pierced through the bones with iron spikes.

It is at such times, when we are in the midst of being hurt, that many of us are the least able to forgive. We would prefer to put a little distance between us and the pain before we are ready to even consider forgiving the other person. This is doubly true when the ones who have

It is at such times, when we are in the midst of being hurt, that many of us are the least able to forgive. We would prefer to put a little distance between us and the pain before we are ready to even consider forgiving the other person.

Healing Through the Power of Prayer

wronged us show no remorse for what they have done.

Yet Jesus freely forgave at the moment when the pain was being inflicted upon him—even as he was being ridiculed by those around him: "Those who passed by derided him, shaking their heads and saying, 'Aha! You who would destroy the temple and build it in three days, save yourself, and come down from the cross!' In the same way the chief priests, along with the scribes, were also mocking him among themselves and saying 'He saved others; he cannot save himself. Let the Messiah, the King of Israel, come down from the cross now, so that we may see and believe.' Those who were crucified with him also taunted him" (Mark 15:29–32).

It is easy to picture these words, dripping with sarcasm and contempt. At one time or another, each of us has experi-enced some form of verbal attack. What we have perhaps not experienced is being wholly unworthy of it, as Jesus was. For us, part of the sting is knowing in our hearts that there may be a grain of truth in the reproach—which neverthe-less may have been amplified, twisted, and used against us. It is the unfairness of such verbal attacks that wound us, and it is then hard to keep things in perspective.

The story is told of a man who felt that he was being unduly criticized by those around him. He was convinced that his colleagues at work were speaking against him behind his back. One day, his inner distress came to a head after what he felt was an unfair rep-rimand by his boss. Driving home that evening, his eyes filled with tears as he poured out his heart to God about the persecution he was experiencing. Then he heard what he took to be his heavenly Father speaking to him: "My son, just be glad they don't know the real truth about you."

Even if we are completely in the right in a particular circumstance, honesty demands that we admit that there have been times when we have hurt and wronged others. Realizing how we would want to be forgiven should make it easier to forgive those who have wronged us.

Jesus was once asked by his disciple Peter how often we are commanded to forgive those who sin against us. "'As many as seven times?' Jesus said to him, 'Not seven times, but, I tell you, seventy-seven times'" (Matthew 18:21–22).

Some of us are dutifully counting and looking forward to finally reaching 77. But that is not Jesus' point. To explain what he means, he tells a parable about a servant who

was been forgiven a very large debt by his master. The man saved himself from being sold into slavery by begging for mercy, which was granted him. The servant's debt was canceled, but he took a different attitude towards those who owed him: "But that same slave, as he went out, came upon one of his fellow slaves who owed him a hundred denarii [i.e., a few dollars]; and seizing him by the throat, he said, 'Pay what you owe.' Then his fellow slave fell down and pleaded with him, 'Have patience with me, and I will pay you.' But he refused; then he went and threw him into prison until he would pay the debt. When his fellow slaves saw what happened, they were greatly distressed, and they went and reported to their lord all that had taken place." (Matthew 18:28–31).

Needless to say, when the man's master learned what he

Healing Through the Power of Prayer

had done, he was furious: "'You wicked slave, I forgave you all that debt because you pleaded with me. Should you not have had mercy on your fellow slave, as I had mercy on you?' And in anger his lord handed him over to be tortured until he would pay his entire debt. So my heavenly Father will also do to every one of you, if you do not forgive your brother or sister from your heart" (verses 32–35).

We can hear these words of Jesus and sincerely desire to obey them—but it is still not easy. And at times we fail—for what may be very understandable reasons—to achieve what Jesus is asking of us in this parable.

The noted Nazi hunter Simon Wiesenthal tells a story about when he was in a Polish concentration camp during the Second World War. One day he was told to clean the rubbish out of a building that was being used as a hospital for wounded soldiers from the Eastern Front. As he was cleaning, a nurse ordered him to follow her. He trailed after her, perplexed at what she would want.

She took him up to a ward where a young German SS

> *We can hear these words of Jesus and sincerely desire to obey them—but it is still not easy. And at times we fail—for what may be very understandable reasons—to achieve what Jesus is asking of us.*

Trooper lay in bed bandaged and dying. The soldier grasped his hand and told him he had to confess his sins to a Jew.

The soldier told about being in a Russian village when a few hundred Jews were rounded up for execution. The Jews were forced into houses that were then set on fire. The soldier related what happened next: "Behind the window of the second floor, I

saw a man with a small child in his arms. His

clothing was alight. By his side stood a woman, doubtless the mother of the child. With his free hand the man covered the child's eyes— then he jumped into the street. Seconds later the mother followed. We shot . . . Oh, God . . . I shall never forget it— it haunts me."

In agony of spirit he continued: "I know that what I told you is terrible. I have longed to talk about it to a Jew and beg forgiveness from him. I know that what I am asking is almost too much, but without your answer I cannot die in peace."[2]

> Corrie Ten Boom traveled the world telling her story of how God had transformed her during her time in the concentration camp. She preached about the power of forgiveness; that it can change even the hardest of hearts.

Healing Through the Power of Prayer

There was a terrible silence as Wiesenthal pondered the man's request. Then, in his own words, he tells of his decision: "I stood up and looked in his direction, at his folded hands. At last I made up my mind and without a word I left the room."[3] The soldier's dying request, to be forgiven by a member of the race he had helped to slaughter, was denied.

And who among us can admonish Simon Wiesenthal for not being able to forgive? Wiesenthal himself was troubled. He continued to be haunted by this incident. Years later he included it in his book *The Sunflower*, asking of his readers at the end: "What would you have done?"[4]

FORGIVING OTHERS

Corrie Ten Boom experienced a similar crisis—she was also asked to forgive the unforgivable. In her book *The Hiding Place*,

she tells her story of being imprisoned along with her father and sister by the Nazis for the crime of harboring Jews. Of the three of them, only Corrie survived the horrors of the concentration camp.

Ten Boom traveled the world telling her story of how God had transformed her during her time in the concentration camp. She preached about the power of forgiveness; that it can change even the hardest of hearts.

Then one day she found herself in Munich, Germany. She was preaching to a people hungry for forgiveness. After the service, a man came up to Ten Boom. He looked familiar. The man reached out his hand to her. "Ja, Fraulein Ten Boom," he said, "I am so glad that Jesus forgives us all of our sin, just as you say."[5]

Healing Through the Power of Prayer

Then she remembered. Once again the feelings of terror and of hatred swept over her. The man had been a guard at the concentration camp. He had humiliated her and the other women by forcing them to shower while he watched, leering at them. As a former SS guard at the camp, he shared the responsibility for the deaths of her beloved father and sister. And now he expected her to forgive him?

Ten Boom froze. Despite all the years spent preaching about forgiving one's enemies, she found it difficult to take her own medicine. When she came face to face with one of those responsible for the deepest wounding of her heart, she could not bring herself to forgive him.

"Jesus, I can't forgive this man. Forgive me," she silently prayed. It was as far as she could go. She did not have the strength to forgive him. But at least she was willing to go halfway—she recognized what she needed to do.[6]

At that moment, God met her and gave her the strength to go the rest of the way. Without realizing it, her hand reached out and took the hand of her former tormentor, forgiving him in Jesus' name.

> The ministry of Corrie Ten Boom has blessed millions around the world because of the love of Christ that radiated from her. Her willingness to forgive released that love.

Healing Through the Power of Prayer

The ministry of Corrie Ten Boom has blessed millions around the world because of the love of Christ that radiated from her. Her willingness to forgive released that love.

In his book *Forgive and Forget*, Lewis Smedes tells about another kind of calamity—one perhaps more familiar in our day. A woman he knows, named Myra Broger, was a promising actress until her career was cut short by a hit-and-run driver who left her severely handicapped.

But that was not the only tragedy: Her husband, also an actor, soon abandoned her. The combination of those two blows would be enough to make anyone bitter—but not Broger. One day, Smedes happened to ask her if she had been able to forgive her husband. Broger answered: "I find myself wishing him well."

Smedes couldn't quite believe her response, so he pressed her: "Suppose you learned today that he had married a sexy, young starlet, could you pray that he would be happy with her?" It was an outrageous thing to ask and he knew it, but Broger didn't take offense. "Yes, I could and I would," she replied genuinely, "Steve needs love very much, and I want him to have it."[7]

We can think that we will forgive. We can shake our heads at a woman who is willing to forgive a man who left her when she was at her lowest point. We can accuse her of being naive: that she is refusing to face up to reality and that she had better get with it and start hating him. But we should ask ourselves: Who is in better emotional shape—Broger or the woman who can't stand her daughter-in-law?

Broger is at peace. It may have come through anguished struggle, but in the end—like

Healing Through the Power of Prayer

Corrie Ten Boom—she chose to relinquish her hate and bitterness—and to forgive.

It may be hard to conceive of ourselves responding like Ten Boom and Broger. We may be bearing burdens that go deeper than the particular incident that hurt us. The wrong we suffered may have stirred up an unresolved emotional wound from our life history. Forgiveness can seem almost impossible when the incident touches and hurts a sore spot on our psyche.

The source of our hurt can often be traced to our childhood. C. S. Lewis struggled almost his entire life to forgive a childhood teacher who humiliated him in front of the other students and made his life almost unbearable. At the end of his life, he wrote to a friend: "Do you know, only a few weeks ago I realized suddenly that I had at last forgiven the cruel schoolmaster who so darkened my childhood. I'd been trying to do it for years; and like you, each time I thought I'd done it, I found, after a week or so it all had to be attempted over again. But this time I feel it is the real thing."[8]

God knows our emotional infirmities. He understands the wounds of our souls better than we ourselves. He knows

> *God knows our emotional infirmities. He understands the wounds of our souls better than we ourselves. He knows we would forgive if we were able.*

Healing Through the Power of Prayer

we would forgive if we were able. And he will help us if, like Corrie Ten Boom, we are willing to meet him halfway.

Despite the atrocities he committed, most of us can find sympathy in our hearts for the dying German soldier who begged forgiveness. When people humble themselves and admit their wrongdoing, our resistance to forgiving them tends to melt away—as it should. The gospels give us a beautiful example of a humbled heart in the woman who had lived a sinful life who came to Jesus when he was dining at the house of Simon the Pharisee. As the woman stood behind him weeping, her tears wet his feet. She wiped his feet with her hair, kissed them, and poured expensive perfume from an alabaster jar on them.

Seeing this, Simon was greatly offended. A Pharisee would never associate with such a sinful person. He criticized Jesus in his heart for allowing a woman of her reputation near him. Knowing what he was thinking, Jesus said to him: "'Do you see this woman? I entered your house; you gave me no water for my feet, but she has bathed my feet with her tears and dried them with her hair. You gave me no kiss, but from the time I came in she has not stopped kissing my feet. You did not anoint my head with oil, but she has anointed my feet with ointment. Therefore, I tell you, her sins, which were many, have been forgiven; hence she has shown great love. But the one to whom little is forgiven, loves little.' Then he said to her, 'Your sins are forgiven.'" (Luke 7:44–48).

What is surprising about this story is who Jesus commended. After all, doesn't living a morally upright life—like the Pharisee surely lived—count

Healing Through the Power of Prayer

for anything? Of course it does. And there is no suggestion here that Jesus takes whatever sins the woman may have committed lightly. But his praise went not to the religious man who was steeped in self-righteousness, but rather to the woman who was broken because of her wrong actions.

Jesus is giving us a crucial truth here: The greater our sense of needing to be forgiven, the greater our capacity to love and forgive others. Which of the two would we find ourselves identifying with?

"Loveless husbands, Nazis, tormenting teachers who scar children for life—maybe Jesus can forgive them but I can't." Many can identify with the sentiment expressed by those words. What can be said to those who cannot bring themselves to forgive human monsters? In Greg Anderson's book *The Triumphant Patient*, a woman with terminal cancer who is wrestling with forgiveness has a conversation with a counselor named Edward: "'How can we possibly forgive some people?' she asked. 'Murderers. Rapists. Child molesters. Recently I heard the story of a father who actually set fire to his son. Are you suggesting that even actions of that kind should be forgiven? How can that be possible?' 'Put the focus on who benefits most from the forgiving,' Edward said. 'We do, the ones who do the forgiving. It's not so much that we let the other person off the hook, but that we let ourselves off the hook and can stop investing all our emotional energy in holding onto perceived wrongs. Our energy can then be directed toward helping heal our entire lives.'"[9]

We sometimes mistakenly believe that by forgiving others, we award them yet another

Healing Through the Power of Prayer

advantage over us. We think we are allowing them to win one more time, while we—poor forgiving saps—are the losers.

Nothing could be further from the truth. Forgiving empowers us by setting us free from the chains of bitterness, resentment, and anger. And we must not forget that by forgiving we are not condoning the other person's actions. God sees everything. The issue of personal retribution should be left to him: "Beloved, never avenge yourselves, but leave room for the wrath of God; for it is written, 'Vengeance is mine, I will repay, says the Lord.' No, 'if your enemies are hungry, feed them; if they are thirsty, give them something to drink; for by doing this you will heap burning coals on their heads.' Do not be overcome by evil, but overcome evil with good" (Romans 12:19–21).

It is a comforting thought to know that we do not have to try to exact revenge for the wrongs done to us. God will repay those responsible in a way that is far

> *Forgiving empowers us by setting us free from the chains of bitterness, resentment, and anger. And we must not forget that by forgiving we are not condoning the other person's actions. God sees everything. The issue of personal retribution should be left to him.*

Healing Through the Power of Prayer

more just than we could accomplish ourselves. In the meantime, our duty, with God's help, is to forgive. And more than that—to have a forgiving heart; so much so that we would even be willing to show kindness to our enemies.

FORGIVING GOD

It is one thing to forgive another human—we might even be able to forgive our enemy. But what do we do when we feel we have suffered the ultimate betrayal—that God has let us down? Most of us, at one time or another, can identify with the midnight cry of the psalmist:

"Will the Lord spurn forever,
    and never again be favorable?
Has his steadfast love ceased
forever?

Are his
promises at
an end for
all time?

Has God forgotten to be
    gracious?
Has he in anger shut up his
    compassion?[11]
(Psalm 77:7–9).

Were it not for the fact that these words are found in Holy Scripture, most of us would not consider the author's attitude very spiritual. These are words that we would share privately and to a privileged few, lest our faith be doubted. It is not often that we hear such honest doubts being voiced from the pulpit.

But maybe they should be, for as Dan B. Allender and Tremper Longman III write in their book *Cry of the Soul*, such words are the plea of faith: "The irony of faith is that it is not a quiet submission to the fates. It asks, and it shouts; it is a cry that is heard in heaven. Faith does not affect pious language, nor does it presume that honest struggle will be smashed in a fit of divine pique. The irony of questioning God is that it honors Him: it turns our hearts away from ungodly despair toward a passionate desire to comprehend Him."[10]

Our theology may agree with the psalmist that "Good and upright is the Lord" (Psalm 25:8), but our experience can make us question. Sometimes we get so low, so desperate, that we feel like taking the advice of Job's wife: "Curse God, and die" (Job 2:9).

It is one thing to forgive another human—we might even be able to forgive our enemy. But what do we do when we feel we have suffered the ultimate betrayal—that God has let us down?

justice: "One day when we came back from work, we saw three gallows rearing up in the assembly place.... Three victims in chains—and one of them the little servant, the sad-eyed angel.... The three victims [were] mounted together onto chairs. The three necks were placed at the same moment within the nooses.... At a sign... the three chairs tipped over. Total silence throughout the camp.... Then the march past began. The two adults were no longer alive.... But the

Yet another Holocaust survivor, Elie Wiesel, tells a story of seeing a little boy die amidst profound questions of God's

Healing Through the Power of Prayer

third rope was still moving; being so light, the child was still alive. For more than half an hour he stayed there, struggling between life and death, dying in slow agony under our eyes. And we had to look him full in the face. Behind me, I heard [a] man asking: 'Where is God now?' And I heard a voice within me answer him: 'Where is he? Here he is—He is hanging here on this gallows.'"[11]

God is not absent from our pain. He is there with us in one way or another. No cry, no tear escapes his notice. After all, he himself has been where we are; he has cried out also, "My God, my God, why have you forsaken me?"

Bridget Meehan, in her book *The Healing Power of Prayer*, tells about a couple whose 17-year-old son was killed in an automobile accident after falling asleep during a late night drive home from a party. His parents were bitter because the other parents did not pick up their children at the party, which made it necessary for their son to drive them home. The parents were unable

> *God is not absent from our pain. He is there with us. No cry, no tear escapes his notice. After all, he himself has been where we are; he has cried out also, "My God, my God, why have you forsaken me?"*

to forgive the other parents until they realized that Jesus shared in their suffering: "After several months of physical and mental anguish, the bereaved father said that he found the strength to forgive at the foot of the Cross of Christ. 'I clung to Christ on the Cross, saw the tears in his eyes, and I knew that he shared my loss. At that moment I forgave, and a burden was lifted from my heart.'"[12]

In this world, we may never know why we are permitted to suffer the wrongs we do—why God does not prevent them. As we have already seen, we live in a world steeped in evil, and in one way or another, we all suffer the effects of that evil. Kelsey writes: "We cannot even foresee how a particular evil will affect us, and there is certainly no easy way to deal with it. Even Jesus was able to deal with evil only by the drastic action of being born among human

beings and being crucified and resurrected. Christians, it seems clear, cannot expect final answers to these questions."[13]

No final answers. We desperately want to know why, but instead we are told:

"Trust in the Lord with all your
   heart,
      and do not rely on your own
      insight.
In all your ways acknowledge
   him,
      and he will make straight
      your paths.
Do not be wise in your own
   eyes;
      fear the Lord, and turn away
      from evil.
It will be healing for your flesh
   and a refreshment for your
      body."
(Proverbs 3:5–8).

Why, instead of being granted the answers to our questions, are we told to trust God? Maybe it is because the tapestry of the divine plan is so infinitely complex as to be beyond our comprehension. Perhaps it is because to unweave such an explanation will require an eternity in heaven.

THE GATEWAY TO HEALING

Father Heron tells of being healed of his long-standing depression during a conference led by Father Francis MacNutt. Father Heron went forward after the mass to receive prayer for healing. As he was being prayed for, something remarkable happened: He slid to the floor and remained there for more than two hours.

Father Heron experienced what is called being "slain in the Spirit," a phenomenon that sometimes occurs to people when they are being prayed for. The individual often appears to faint, but in reality they remain conscious of the presence of the Holy Spirit.

Some claim that being "slain in the Spirit" is not a valid experience for a Christian because the Bible does not explicitly mention such a practice. But argument is a weak one, and especially in this case because we simply do not know all of the ways in which God worked in the time of the New Testament. Only a fraction of the miracles that Jesus and his followers performed were recorded, as John states in his gospel: "But there are also many other things that Jesus did; if every one of them were written down, I suppose that the world itself could not contain the books that would be written" (John 21:25).

We have seen some of the many ways in which Jesus healed and that his means of dealing with people cannot be reduced to an exact formula or technique. The apostles also were channels of healing in

Healing Through the Power of Prayer

remarkable and unusual ways. The Book of Acts records that "many signs and wonders were done among the people through the apostles," so much so that we read: "so that they even carried out the sick into the streets, and laid them on cots and mats, in order that Peter's shadow might fall on some of them as he came by. A great number of people would also gather from the towns around Jerusalem, bringing the sick and those tormented by unclean spirits, and they were all healed" (Acts 5:12,15–16).

> *W*hy, instead of being granted the answer to our questions, are we told to trust God? Maybe it is because the tapestry of the divine plan is so infinitely complex as to be beyond our comprehension.

Apparently the sick hoped that if Peter's shadow fell on them, they would be healed. While we do not know why they believed this would work, they must have had some basis for their expectation. We have also seen how God used such unusual means as handkerchiefs to bring healing.

So it should not come as a surprise that in the midst of being prayed for, some people are overcome with the sense of God's presence. There is, of course, always a caution when people observe or learn about such an experience and

Healing Through the Power of Prayer

earnestly desire it for themselves—they may unwittingly "fake" it.

This, however, was not what happened to Father Heron, since he did not seek the experience nor did he expect that it would happen to him. He relates what happened while he was resting on the floor: "During that time I not only realized that I had not forgiven certain people, a fact that I was not aware of before, but I also learned more about the nature and demands of Christian forgiveness while lying on the ground there than I had ever understood from talks or books. The Holy Spirit gave me a much deeper insight on this subject, which I regard as one of the major spiritual blessings of my life."[14]

The evil in the world has affected each of us in different ways; each of us has been hurt. And our responses are not always like that of Myra Broger or Corrie Ten Boom. Rather than learn to forgive, we often find it easier to blame others or even God. These unhealthy responses

> *Rather than learn to forgive, we often find it easier to blame others or even God. These unhealthy responses to our pain build up within our psyche. On a conscious level, we may even succeed in forgetting those situations that we have been unable to forgive.*

to our pain build up within our psyche. We may even succeed in forgetting those situations that we have been unable to forgive.

But just as dirt swept under a rug does not go away, on a subconscious level, the issues that we have not dealt with continue to affect us. They may re-emerge as negative emotions such as depression, anger, bitterness, and resentment. They may lead to unhealthy behavior or health problems, or they may poison our relationships with those we love. Repressed negative emotions will surely sap our joy.

It is no exaggeration to state, as Father Heron does: "To repent of our pride and to grow in humility can be very healing emotionally, and can transform painful memories of the past. Forgiveness is the key to much or even most inner healing."[15]

Jesus often spoke of forgiveness in his parables and in his teachings. He taught his disciples and his followers to pray: "Forgive us our debts, as we also have forgiven our debtors" (Matthew 6:12). And, ultimately, he modeled forgiveness when he prayed on the cross: "Father, forgive them; for they do not know what they are doing" (Luke 23:34).

We are not to forgive only when it is convenient for us or when the other person has prostrated themselves sufficiently before us. Forgiveness is not meant only for those who hurt us unintentionally, but also for those who intentionally harmed us.

Perhaps the greatest challenge of all is to learn to forgive ourselves for how we have harmed ourselves and others. The reason is one of pride: We cannot bring ourselves to accept that we could be capable of such a despicable act. If someone else commits the offense, at least our self-esteem is intact. But it can be very difficult to face up to the fact that we ourselves are sometimes the guilty party.

We can magnify our failures, considering ourselves contemptible and worse than others. But this is to deny the universal truth that "all have sinned and fall short of the glory of God" (Romans 3:23). The good news is that Jesus came to bring physical, emotional, and spiritual healing to people like us. Luke the physician records his

words: "Those who are well have no need of a physician, but those who are sick; I have come to call not the righteous but sinners to repentance" (Luke 5:31).

It is when we have a sense of being forgiven that we can fulfill Jesus' command "You shall love your neighbor as yourself" (Matthew 19:19). Only when we have a healthy concept of who we are in the eyes of our Creator can we reach out in love to those around us— even our enemies.

The alternative, to refuse to accept forgiveness for ourselves and others, can lead to physical and emotional health problems. Doctors have long known that those who are experiencing the death of a loved one, divorce, or the

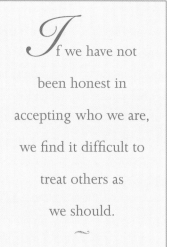

If we have not been honest in accepting who we are, we find it difficult to treat others as we should.

Healing Through the Power of Prayer

loss of a job are at heightened risk for cancer or a heart attack. In such trying circumstances, there can be much anger, resentment, and unforgiveness. There are often feelings of lonliness as well.

During such difficult times, those who have not learned forgiveness can also engage in manipulative behavior toward others—and even God. If

we have not been honest in accepting who we are, we find it difficult to treat others as we should. We can even use prayer as a way of manipulating God.

~ 207 ~
Healing Through the Power of Prayer

CHAPTER 14:
Wrong Motives

You ask and do not receive,
because you ask wrongly, in order
to spend what you get on
your pleasures.

James 4:3

In his book *Prayer Is Good Medicine*, Dr. Larry Dossey tells about a young man who, like all red-blooded Americans, earnestly desired to own his own wheels. So he prayed for a car. Nothing happened. He prayed a few more times and still no car. Then he realized that God did not work that way, so he decided to try another tact: He stole a car and prayed for forgiveness.[1]

Sometimes we treat God like a cosmic Santa Claus.

We dictate what he should give us and bristle at the suggestion that he might actually know what is best and have other plans for us. Frankly, we are not too interested in those plans because we fear it may entail some great sacrifice on our part.

Does this sound too harsh? Sometimes those who are outside the fold see the foibles of Christians all too clearly. The novelist Aldous Huxley, no professed believer himself, cut to the heart of our self-serving prayers: "To acquire the knack

Healing Through the Power of Prayer

of getting his petitions answered, a man does not have to know or love God. . . . All that he requires is a burning sense of the importance of his own ego and its own desires, coupled with a firm conviction that there exists, out there in the universe, something not himself which can be wheedled or dragooned into satisfying those desires. If I repeat 'Thy will be done,' with the necessary degree of faith and persistency, the chances are that sooner or later and somehow or other, I shall get what I want. Whether my will coincides with that of God, and whether in getting what I want I shall get what is spiritually, morally or even materially good for me are questions which I cannot answer in advance. Only time and eternity will show. . . . The third clause of the Lord's Prayer is repeated daily by millions,

who have not the slightest intention of letting any will be done, except their own."[2]

Before we chuckle and dismiss what Huxley is saying, let us stop for a moment of reflection: Is there any truth in this harsh indictment? In our hearts, many of us would be forced to admit that this is the attitude behind our prayers. According to the Book of James, this is one reason why our prayers sometimes go unanswered: "You do not have, because you do not ask. You ask and do not receive, because you ask wrongly, in order to spend what you get on your pleasures" (James 4:2–3).

Just as we can have wrong motives in what we ask for, there can also be wrong motives in what we refuse to ask for. We can choose to

Healing Through the Power of Prayer

remain sick and not to seek healing. It begins when we are children, when many of us learned how to use sickness to get out of doing something. If we didn't want to go to school, we could imagine a headache into existence or translate our blue feelings into a cold. How easily the exclamation "my head hurts!" relieved us of the dreaded tedium of the day.

Of course, we were clever enough not to try it too often lest our mothers catch on. But once in a while, it worked like a charm. So we retained the selective use of sickness for our own purposes—and the odd thing about it is that we actually felt physically ill.

For others, the causes that trigger illness are not so benign. Small children are not able to defend themselves against emotional or physical abuse, and this hurt and dejection may take the form of physical illness. Other behavior, like chronic bed wetting, can be a child's subliminal protest against a high level of tension in the home or some unfulfilled emotional need.

The pattern of behavior continues as the child grows older. In high school and college, a

> *Just as we can have wrong motives in what we ask for, there can also be wrong motives in what we refuse to ask for. We can choose to remain sick and not to seek healing.*

bout with the flu strikes at exam time or just before a term paper deadline—giving us a few days reprieve. As we grow older, sickness can remain our subconscious safety valve to relieve us of unwanted responsibilities or to get people to do what we want them to do.

Kenneth L. Bakken and Kathleen H. Hofeller ask: "Is getting sick the only way you can justify taking time off from work, family, and social responsibilities? Does it seem to be the only way to get attention and nurturing? Many of us are at least dimly aware of these secondary gains. Good health involves being aware of our needs and being able to communicate them to others. Chronic illness creates special problems including whole new roles and patterns of interaction and dependency. Once established, these patterns become resistant to change."[3]

Sick people get special treatment. People are nicer, kinder to them. Others do favors for them and do not expect them to assume the obligations of healthy people. Still, most people would gladly trade all this for the chance to be healed.

Others, however, secretly dread the loss of attention and special consideration that their illness brings them. If they were healed, they would have to be treated like ordinary people. It might also mean that they might not get their way, as Morton Kelsey writes: "Most of us know at least a little about such illness. Most of us have known some person who never married because mama's heart invariably went bad at the sight of an eligible partner. Or if we have had any real neurotic trouble ourselves—and my experience is that most people fall into this class—we have probably thought at some time or another, 'If only I could be just sick enough to get off the hook!' And perhaps our body has in fact granted our wish."[4]

Whether or not we are aware of it, we can sometimes use illness to manipulate others. Rather than express our desires in a normal fashion and take the chance that others may not accede to our wishes, we "stack the deck" in our favor with illness. Our family and friends are more likely to give in if they pity us.

In their text *Psychosomatic Medicine*, authors Edward Weiss and O. Spurgeon English tell of a young woman who began suffering from severe headaches, which became steadily worse. She developed intestinal complications and had to be hospitalized. The doctors were at a loss for a diagnosis until an old physician was called in. He wisely questioned her about her life and quickly discovered the problem. The girl's older brother, who supported the family, had recently become engaged to be married. She wished her brother the best but was all too well aware of the upheaval it would cause in her family situation. Her body registered its opposition by becoming ill. Once she became aware of the dynamics of her illness, she promptly recovered.

Let there be no mistake: Illnesses that arise from emotional difficulties are just as real—and as serious—as any other. The psychosomatic causes of illness have been known to physicians since time immemorial. In his classic work *Psychology and Religion*, renowned psychologist Carl Jung relates the following examples from his own practice: "Since my readers may not be familiar with these medical facts I may instance a case of hysterical fever, with a temperature of 102

Healing Through the Power of Prayer

degrees, which was cured in a few minutes through confession of the psychological cause. A patient [had] psoriasis extending over practically the whole body. . . . After six weeks of intense analysis and discussion of his purely psychological difficulties, there came about as an unexpected by-product, the almost complete disappearance of the skin disease. In another case, the patient had recently undergone an operation for distention of the colon. Forty centimeters of it had been removed, but this was followed by another extraordinary distention. . . . As soon as certain intimate psychological facts were discovered, the colon began to function normally again."[5]

Just because an illness has a psychological origin, however, does not mean that it is any less real. If we suspect such a cause for someone's illness, we should not take it any less seriously.

We must not underestimate the power of our emotions to affect our body. Each of us has at some time and in some way been hurt by others. We can decide to allow the hurt and fear to work their destructive effects upon our lives. Or with God's help we can choose the hard path of forgiveness that leads to freedom.

> *Let there be no mistake: Illnesses that arise from emotional difficulties are just as real—and as serious— as any other.*

Healing Through the Power of Prayer

CHAPTER 15: A Thorn in the Flesh

> But he said to me, "my grace is sufficient for you, for power is made in perfect weakness." So, I will boast all the more gladly of my weaknesses, so that the power of Christ may dwell in me.
>
> 2 Corinthians 12:9

If anyone was qualified to be an expert on miracles and healing, it would be the Apostle Paul. Not only had he healed others, but he had experienced the miraculous in his own life. The Book of Acts relates how  Paul was badly injured and left for dead: "Jews came there from Antioch and Iconium and won over the crowds. Then they stoned Paul and dragged him out of the city, supposing that he was dead. But when the disciples surrounded him, he got up and went into the city" (Acts 14:19–20).

It is not clear here whether Paul had actually died or not, but either way he must have experienced a miraculous healing. Stoning was a serious business and usually fatal. But even if he had only lost consciousness, he had been at least severely injured.

On another occasion, a young man fell asleep while Paul was preaching. He fell from the third story and was picked up dead: "Paul went down, and bending over him took him in his arms, and said, 'Do not be alarmed, for his life is in him.' Then Paul went upstairs, and after he had broken bread and eaten, he continued to converse with them until dawn; then he left. Meanwhile they had taken the boy away alive and were not a little comforted" (Acts 20:10–12).

After being shipwrecked on the island of Malta, Paul experienced another miraculous healing after an attack from a potentially lethal serpent. "Paul had gathered a bundle of brushwood and was putting it on the fire, when a viper, driven

out by the heat, fastened itself on his hand. . . . He, however, shook off the creature into the fire and suffered no harm. They were expecting him to swell up or drop dead, but after they had waited a long time and saw nothing happened to him, they changed their minds and began to say that he was a god" (Acts 28:3–6).

We then read that Paul healed the father of the chief official of Malta, along with many others: "After this happened, the rest of the people on the island who had diseases also came and were cured" (verse 9).

Paul believed in healing; he experienced healing in his own life and in the lives of others. He also taught the churches in his care to practice healing. In

Healing Through the Power of Prayer

his letter to the church in Corinth, he includes the "gifts of healing" (1 Corinthians 12:9) in his list of spiritual gifts. Thus, it is all the more puzzling to learn that both Paul and his associates suffered maladies that were not healed.

His trusted lieutenant Timothy had recurring stomach problems, for which Paul offered some advice: "No longer drink only water, but take a little wine for the sake of your stomach and your frequent ailments" (1 Timothy 5:23). A bit of advice about drinking wine seems a pale substitute for physical healing. Why didn't Paul just heal his accomplice? In a later letter to Timothy, he states simply that "Trophimus I left ill in Miletus" (2 Timothy 4:20).

What's going on here? Did Paul lose his healing touch—or had he become unspiritual? The question becomes even more puzzling when we read Paul's own problem: "Therefore, to keep me from being too elated, a thorn was given me in the flesh, a messenger of Satan to torment me, to keep me from being too elated. Three times I appealed to the Lord about this, that it would leave me, but he said to me, 'My grace is sufficient for you, for power is made perfect in weakness'" (2 Corinthians 12:7–9).

How could it be that someone like Paul, who experienced such dramatic miracles, could fail to find healing in his own life? There are no easy answers, and Paul's thorn in the flesh has truly become a thorn in the side for theologians.

Some try to avoid the issue of why Paul was not healed by claiming his thorn was a spiritual temptation, not a physical problem. But we read in Galatians that Paul indeed did suffer from physical illness: "You

Healing Through the Power of Prayer

know that it was because of a physical infirmity that I first announced the gospel to you; though my condition put you to the test, you did not scorn or despise me" (Galatians 4:13–14).

Scholars have suggested various ideas as to what Paul's thorn in the flesh was. One prominent theory is that he suffered from a disease of the eyes. We have an indication of this in the same Galatian passage when he says: "For I testify that, had it been possible, you would have torn out your eyes and given them to me" (verse 15). He commends the church in Galatia for being willing to sacrifice their own eyes for his eyes.

At the end of his letter to the Galatians, he makes the following comment: "See what large letters I make when I am writing in my own hand!" (6:11). This is another indication that his sight may not have been good and that he had to print large letters to see what he was writing. Some speculate his eye problems may have originated

> *H*ow could it be that someone like Paul, who experienced such dramatic miracles, could fail to find healing in his own life? There are no easy answers, and Paul's thorn in the flesh has truly become a thorn in the side for theologians.

Healing Through the Power of Prayer

when he had been temporarily blinded during his conversion experience on the road to Damascus (see Acts 9).

That is just about the sum total of the evidence. It will probably never be determined with certainty what Paul's ailment really was. But he does tell us the purpose for his thorn in the flesh; it was given to him to prevent him "from being too elated."

The first thing to be noted here is that Paul's thorn in the flesh was not given to him as punishment for sin. He does not say: "I became elated . . . and was punished by my infirmity." We have seen that physical sickness can result from wrong actions—but it is by no means always the case. Much illness can be attributed to the unavoidable effects of living in a fallen world.

But there are still other reasons, one of which is indicated by Paul here. Frankly put, his illness was given to him to keep him humble.

The argument "How dare God make someone suffer just to keep them humble!" is admittedly an argument with strong emotional appeal. But it shows that we do not place much value on humility. And it doesn't help to live in a culture that worships power and success, while despising meekness. *Nice guys finish last!* is a popular expression that we've all heard. The message is clear: Humility means weakness.

Or does it? Paul was convinced that the exact opposite was true. He believed that the humility that his physical weakness brought was actually the source of his spiritual strength: "So, I will boast all the more gladly of my weaknesses, so that the power of Christ may dwell in me. Therefore I am content in weaknesses, insults, hardships, persecutions, and calamities for the sake of Christ; for whenever I am weak, then I am strong" (2 Corinthians 12:9–10).

Few of us could wholeheartedly echo Paul's sentiments here, and even fewer would choose to experience the tribulations he went through. His attitude of gratefulness is all the more amazing when we read the catalog of his sufferings: "But whatever anyone dares to boast of—I am speaking as a fool—I also dare to boast of that. . . . Are they ministers of Christ? I am talking like a madman—I am a better one: with far greater labors, far more imprisonments, with countless floggings, and often near death. Five times I have received from the Jews the forty lashes minus one. Three times I was beaten with rods. Once I received a stoning. Three times I was shipwrecked; for a night and a day I was adrift at sea; on frequent journeys, in danger from rivers, danger from bandits . . . hungry and thirsty, often without food, cold and naked" (2 Corinthians 11:21–27).

Reading this list should forever put to rest the notion

> *Therefore I am content in weaknesses, insults, hardships, persecutions, and calamities for the sake of Christ; for whenever I am weak, then I am strong.*
>
> 2 Corinthians 12:10

Healing Through the Power of Prayer

that sickness is the result of a lack of faith or some spiritual weakness. Were the Apostle Paul to stand before us, which of us would dare suggest that if he would only have had more "faith" he would not have had a thorn in the flesh?

In addition to all his afflictions, God permitted Paul to be tormented by a thorn in the flesh even though he pleaded three times for it to be removed. If someone of Paul's stature suffered so, we can be assured, we will also.

REDEMPTIVE SUFFERING

In his ministry and teaching, Jesus presents us with the paradox of healing and suffering. On the one hand, he freely

healed those who came to him. He announced the kingdom of God will ultimately triumph over the forces of evil and death—and he was profoundly moved by the effects of that evil. The shortest verse in the Bible, "Jesus wept," tells us of his heartfelt emotions as he approached the tomb of his friend Lazarus. We have every indication that he desires us to be healthy and whole.

Yet discipleship is not without cost. We are also told: "If any want to become my followers, let them deny themselves and take up their cross daily and follow me. For those who want to save their life will lose it, and those who lose their life for my sake will save it" (Luke 9:23–24).

Take up our cross. The words have no positive association; for most people, they refer only to suffering in an extreme sense. The worst fear of a Jew in the first century was to meet one's end hanging on a cross. Why would Jesus say such a thing, we ask?

It may be that, like the Apostle Paul, suffering is necessary to bring about vital spiritual growth in all of us, as Meehan writes in *The Healing Power of Prayer*: "Physical or emotional illness can be part of God's plan. Sometimes it challenges our complacency in matters of religion and restores our priorities in life. Sometimes sickness, suffering, or pain causes us to change our direction in life so that God may truly be the focus of all human endeavors. Such a change

of heart can be seen in the apostle Paul who was blinded en route to Damascus and, as a result of this misfortune, discovered that the Lord called him to a radical conversion—a total change of direction."[1]

As we have noted, Paul may have suffered the effects of his temporary blindness for the remainder of his life. His thorn in the flesh—whatever it was—

> *If* any want to become my followers, let them deny themselves and take up their cross daily and follow me. For those who want to save their life will lose it, and those who lose their life for my sake will save it.
>
> Luke 9:23–24

was one way God chose for him to carry his cross.

Here is an intriguing question: Suppose Paul would have found a physician who could cure his infirmity? Ephesus, for example, where he ministered and founded a church, was famous for its eye salve. What if that divine barrier were removed? What would have happened to the man who contributed so much to our understanding of our faith?

It is difficult—even terrible—to suffer, just as it is awful to come under the surgeon's knife. But if the physician is not permitted to excise the cancer, all will be lost.

But surely God could find a way of changing us without inflicting pain? Yes, in innumerable ways he surely does. But there are times when stronger medicine is necessary to effect the desired cure, and it will likely involve pain.

Our nervous system is designed to warn us that something is wrong: The loss of pain sensation is a serious, life-threatening condition because the patient is not aware

> But surely God could find a way of changing us without inflicting pain? Yes, in innumerable ways he surely does. But there are times when stronger medicine is necessary to effect the desired cure, and it will likely involve pain.

Healing Through the Power of Prayer

of suffering bodily damage. Likewise, suffering can help us stay sensitive to God's presence and away from that which would cause spiritual harm.

We should also keep in mind that our life here is transitory—the prelude to what lies beyond. Meehan writes: "Suffering and inner woundedness also remind us that we are pilgrims on a journey to eternity. This world is not a lasting home; pain reminds us that we are still on the way to our eternal home. No amount of prayer for physical or inner healing will be able to alleviate all our emptiness and struggle; the Cross is a reality in every Christian's journey."[2]

While few of us would willingly choose redemptive suffering, it is—or will be—a fact of life for most of us. But we need not despair of what may lie ahead, for as Corrie Ten Boom was fond of saying, "The very best is yet to come!"

Part V:

The Big Picture

Then Jesus went with them to a place called Gethsemane; and he said to his disciples, "Sit here while I go over there and pray." He took with him Peter and the two sons of Zebedee, and began to be grieved and agitated. Then he said to them, "I am deeply grieved, even to death; remain here, and stay awake with me." And going a little farther, he threw himself on the ground and prayed, "My Father, if it is possible, let this cup pass from me; yet not what I want but what you want."

Matthew 26:36-39

Healing Through the Power of Prayer

CHAPTER 16: Through the Valley

> We know that all things work
> together for good for those who
> love God, who are called according
> to his purpose.
>
> Romans 8:28

Marjorie Holmes, in her book *To Help You Through the Hurting*, tells of receiving a remarkable letter from a woman named Barbara. The letter was composed at 3 A.M., after Barbara had read something Holmes had written on grief and dying.

As she read what Holmes had  to say about the subject of pain, Barbara commented: "You've been pretty terrific so far, but my dear you are not going to teach me a thing about pain. Or death."[1]

Barbara had recently endured her own private trial by fire, having suffered the loss of five loved ones in the course of a month. There had been a terrible fire. Barbara's 29-year-old sister, six-months pregnant, was burned to death along with her two daughters. Barbara loved those precious girls, aged six and eight, as her own.

Her sister's husband was also horribly burned, but it seemed that he would make it. He rallied, coming out of the coma and sitting up, taking some food. Unable to speak, he wrote one word with his finger: "Wife?" The doctors decided they could not withhold the truth.

The burden was too great for him. He faltered and was gone. But tragedy was not finished. Barbara's father, overcome by his own grief, died of a massive heart attack a week later.

Inconsolable, Barbara sought help in dealing with her great loss. Reading Holmes's book, she reacted strongly: "I wanted to fling your stupid book across the room. Again the words lunged at me, 'Thank you, God, for every cross I have ever had to carry. . .' My God, my God, I cannot thank you for this pain! If I thank you for it, then I must release it to you, and this I

cannot do! To survive, I must keep it and hug it to me. It is mine! I paid for it!"[2]

Barbara says she then stopped writing, got up, and paced the room. She knew what she had to do. She could not go on like this forever. The struggle that Barbara experienced is palpable as she writes: "I went to the kitchen cupboard, laid your book on it, and read it aloud again: 'Thank you, God, for every cross I have ever had to bear. For every honest tear I have ever shed.' No, Lord, I cannot. But I must. And I did. I *actually did!* I released the whole mess to the Father, the Heavenly Father. Because I was paying for the pain all in vain. *Christ had already done it for me.*"[3]

When she surrendered her grief to God, it did not go away. The pain of the loss would

Healing Through the Power of Prayer

always be with her, as it should be; that is the mark of love. But releasing her grief allowed the healing process to begin.

And Barbara was able to catch a glimpse—however imperfect and blurred by her tears—of the big picture: the divine purpose for human existence. She asked herself: "I knew and loved these people; they loved me. Would *I rather not have known them at all?* Oh, God, of course not! My last living memory of Sherry, the youngest, is running down the hall to me with her arms out-stretched, shouting, just because she felt like it, 'Auntie Barbie, I love you, I love you!'

The tears are streaming down my face as I write this. But for the first time in four years, they are tears of joy and acceptance."[4]

Would I rather not have known them at all? The old adage expresses an eternal truth, "It is better to have loved and lost, than never to have loved at all."

Yes, certainly, this assurance will not take away the unbearable loss of a perfectly formed six-month-old baby girl who

> *W*hen she surrendered her grief to God, it did not go away. The pain of the loss would always be with her, as it should be; that is the mark of love. But releasing her grief allowed the healing process to begin.

Healing Through the Power of Prayer

never had a chance at life. But when combined with our expectations for the future, it is a very real hope.

King David faced a similar loss when his newborn son by Bathsheba lay mortally ill: "On the seventh day the child died. . . . Then David rose from the ground, washed, anointed himself, and changed his clothes. He went into the house of the Lord and worshiped; he then went to his own house; and when he asked, they set food before him and he ate. Then his servants said to him, 'What is this thing that you have done? You fasted and wept for the child while it was alive; but when the child died, you rose and ate food.' He said, 'While the child was still alive, I fasted and wept; for I said, "Who knows? The Lord may be gracious to me, and the child may live." But now he is dead, why should I fast? Can I bring him back again? I shall go to him, but he will not return to me'" (2 Samuel 12:18,20–22).

I shall go to him, but he will not return to me. David's response was not that of someone who was callused to his grief or unable to face it. He had a firm expectation of one day being reunited with his child. It gave him the strength to go on with his life. The Apostle Paul speaks of this future hope when he writes to the church at Thessalonica: "But we do not want you to be uninformed, brothers and sisters, about those who have died, so that you may not grieve as others do who have no hope. For since we believe that Jesus died and rose again, even so, through Jesus, God will bring with him those who have died" (1 Thessalonians 4:13–14).

Those who have experienced the death of a loved one are entitled to grieve. It takes

Healing Through the Power of Prayer

months, even years, for the healing. Unfortunately, Western society tends to be uncomfortable around those who are mourning their losses. We tend to short-circuit the grieving process with thoughtless comments such as, "Just be thankful, dear, that his suffering is over." We soon become impatient with the mourner and cannot resist the gentle admonition, "She's already been gone a year—don't you think you ought to be getting on with your life?" Sometimes we avoid the mourner altogether in order to hide our own emotions.

Gradually, at their own pace and at their own time, those who grieve will begin to lift their gaze from the deep valley to the mountains beyond and dare to hope again. They do so because they come to believe that all is not in vain—that there remains a purpose for their lives.

THE MASTER PLAN

How much easier it would be to bear the burdens of our lives if we could have this assurance on a day-to-day basis—that our existence is part of a grand divine plan that remains hidden to us. This is exactly what Paul states in his epistle to the Romans: "We know that all things work together for good for those who love God, who are called according to his purpose. . . . If God is for us, who is against us? He who did not withhold his own Son, but gave him up for all of us, will he not with him also give us everything else?" (Romans 8:28,31–32).

All things work together for good for those who love God. But what is Paul telling us here? Experience teaches us that this does not mean we will never experience pain or suffering. But as Roberta Andreson's story will show, it could mean that we

Healing Through the Power of Prayer

will be spared a greater evil: the loss of the purpose that our Creator has intended for our lives.

As told in the anthology *Chicken Soup for the Surviving Soul*, almost overnight Andreson's life was turned upside down by a near-fatal illness. The year was 1970; Andreson was 23 years old. A mother of three children under the age of three, cancer was the last thing on her mind. Then came the disquieting symptoms and the visit to her doctor, followed in rapid succession by the medical tests and finally the diagnosis: Andreson had fibrosarcoma of the chest wall. It was a dangerous, fast-growing form of cancer that threatened to envelope her heart. The doctors would have to operate immediately.

It had all happened so fast. A shocked Andreson cried out:

"My God, what am I supposed to do? I have three small babies at home and a whole life ahead of me. I don't have time for this, nor do I want to be so frightened. Please don't tell me I am going to die. Please don't tell me that I am going to suffer beyond anything that I could imagine. Please don't take my world away from me and replace it with a living hell until such time as I exist no longer on this earth."[5]

> *We* know that all things work together for good for those who love God, who are called according to his purpose.
>
> Romans 8:28

Healing Through the Power of Prayer

Following 11 hours of surgery, the tumor was removed, leaving Andreson with an incision from the front of her chest all the way around to her back. Her left arm was useless and her lung was deflated and pierced by tubes. Her doctors gave her two months to live and told her they would do everything they could to make her as comfortable as possible.

Two months! Andreson in physical and mental anguish, returned home. But she was determined not to give up. Two months came and went—then

six, then a year. After a decade, Andreson was declared free of cancer. There were no "magic bullet" treatments to take the credit: In those days, doctors had less experience with chemo- and radiation therapy.

> *The path that God chose for her was one that led through the valley of the shadow of death. And it was not a path that she would have chosen for herself.*

Andreson's life has been one of constant pain, as she suffers from recurrent injuries and scar tissue. But she does not regret what she has learned through it all: "I have attempted to take the loss and destruction that cancer caused me and turn it around. All of what I have been through made me strong beyond my years and tolerant of the many acts of life that usually elicit anger. . . . Because

Healing Through the Power of Prayer

of cancer, I learned to enjoy, respect, achieve, console, know great fulfillment and gain extreme insight into what is really important in this life."[6]

Andreson did not experience a miraculous healing. The path that God chose for her was one that led through the valley of the shadow of death. And it was not a path that she would have chosen for herself. Still, she can confess: "Many times I have said, 'I have been truly blessed throughout my life because of the dreaded disease of cancer.'"[7]

Healing Through the Power of Prayer

CHAPTER 17:
The Way Home

He will wipe every tear from their eyes. Death will be no more; mourning and crying and pain will be no more, for the first things have passed away.

Revelation 21:4

To each person experiencing it, every tragedy has its own unique suffering. But while there is no way to compare and rate the adversities people face, there is surely no greater burden than that which Joni Eareckson Tada has borne.

Millions have been touched by Joni's story as told through her book *Joni* and the film by  the same name. In 1967, while a teenager, a diving acci-

dent shattered Joni's life, leaving her a quadriplegic, paralyzed from the shoulders down. It is difficult to imagine the devastation of the youthful, active Joni when she realized she would never walk again, would never experience feeling in over 90 percent of her body.

And it doesn't always get easier as time goes by. In her book, *Heaven—Your Real Home,* Joni expresses her continuing anguish: "I can't tell you how much sorrow I've held at bay over the years. Tears could come easily if I allowed myself to think of all the pleasures of movement and sensation I've missed. Diving into a pool and feeling my arms and legs slice through the water. Plucking guitar strings with my fingers. Jogging till my muscles burn. Cracking steam-broiled Maryland crabs with a mallet. Throwing back the covers in the morning and hopping out of bed. Running my hands across my husband's chest and feeling it. To think that one day we shall hear these words uttered that haven't been spoken since Adam was thrust out of Eden: 'There shall be no more sorrow.'"[1]

Confined for the past three decades in a wheelchair, Joni continues to dream of the kind of everyday physical activities that most of us take for granted. And yet, as much as she misses them, she realizes that her tragic accident has

wrought changes that might not have occurred otherwise: "Hardships are God's way of helping me to get my mind on the hereafter. And I don't mean the hereafter as a death wish, psychological crutch, or escape from reality. I mean 'hereafter' as the true reality. And nothing beats rehearsing a few time-honored, well-worn verses of Scripture if you want to put reality into perspective."[2]

Meditating on the Scriptures can encourage us and fortify us against sinking in the mire of our present circumstances. Verses that seems created just for people like Joni with physical disabilities are 2 Corinthians 4:16–18: "So we do not lose heart. Even though our outer nature is wasting away, our inner nature is being renewed day by day. For this slight

Healing Through the Power of Prayer

momentary affliction is preparing us for an eternal weight of glory beyond all measure, because we look not at what can be seen but at what cannot be seen; for what can be seen is temporary, but what cannot be seen is eternal."

This slight momentary affliction. These words were penned by one who suffered not only from his own thorn in the flesh but from numerous dangers and tribulations. As has been already noted, on various occasions the Apostle Paul was imprisoned, flogged, stoned, and left for dead.

Paul also mentions that: "Five times I have received from the Jews the forty lashes minus

> *So we do not lose heart. Even though our outer nature is wasting away, our inner nature is being renewed day by day.*
>
> 2 Corinthians 4:16

one" (2 Corinthians 11:24). This is stated almost in passing and matter-of-factly, without further comment. Receiving "forty lashes minus one" was a particularly gruesome punishment used by both the Jews and the Romans. The whip used for administering the blows had jagged pieces of glass or metal imbedded in it that would tear into the victim's skin. Great care was taken not to exceed the limit of 40 lashes, for if by accident the soldier administered too many strokes, he would then be liable to receive 40 lashes himself. To avoid that danger, the tradition arose of giving out only 39 lashes.

This brutal form of punishment sometimes proved fatal to the victim. Paul endured it not once but an almost unheard-of five times. And yet he could refer to his "slight momentary affliction"! He could do so because he had his sights set on his heavenly home—an "eternal weight of glory beyond all measure."

It is this hope that keeps Joni going as she suffers the pain, drudgery, and indignity of confinement in a wheelchair: "Somewhere in my broken, paralyzed body is the seed of what I shall become. The paralysis makes what I am to become all the more grand when you contrast atrophied, useless legs against splendorous resurrected legs. I'm convinced if there are mirrors in heaven (and why not?), the images I'll see will be unmistakably 'Joni,' although a much better, brighter 'Joni.' So much so, that it's not worth comparing."[3]

Joni has helped countless thousands to find new hope in the midst of their afflictions. One of these was a young woman named Lisa who was severely paralyzed in an automobile accident. If one could imagine a fate worse than that of Joni, Lisa would be it. Completely paralyzed from her neck down, Lisa could not breathe without a respirator. Her needs too great for her family to care for and all but abandoned by her friends, it seemed that Lisa would be condemned to live out the rest of her life in a nursing home.

She called Joni, who heard the wheezing of Lisa's respirator as she labored to ask Joni why God didn't take her home to heaven now.[4]

Lisa's logic seemed irrefutable. Tragically, it did make sense that if there was any goodness left in God, he would put an end to her suffer-

Healing Through the Power of Prayer

ing. Joni wondered how she could possibly encourage this young woman who was even more paralyzed than she was. But she knew that if anyone could speak to Lisa, she— Joni—would be the one. It was worth a try.

Joni spent the next hour trying to lift Lisa's sights beyond her seemingly hopeless circumstances. She reminded her that paraplegics have one great advantage in that they can more easily obey the command: "Be still, and know that I am God" (Psalm 46:10). The enforced stillness for paraplegics can give them a spiritual receptivity that others do not have. Joni encouraged Lisa to use her time to pray— and to listen to the still, small voice of God speaking to her heart. Her words fell on responsive

ears: "Lisa told me she would start doing just that, especially when I told her that the faintest prayers of those who suffer reach more deeply into God's heart. At that point, I imagined angels in heaven kicking up their heels and rejoicing. This vent-dependent quadriplegic who will lie in bed and spend long moments in prayer may not realize it, but she will be doing the work of angels. After all, there are angels in heaven who do nothing but praise God, such as the seraphim who proclaim day and night before the Lord, 'Holy, Holy, Holy!'"[5]

Joni knew that Lisa had a long and difficult road ahead, and she made a point of keeping in touch. The years passed, and she gradually lost contact with Lisa. But that was not the last contact she would have with her quadriplegic friend: "This year, however, I got the shock of my life when,

Healing Through the Power of Prayer

after I finished speaking at a conference, a young woman hooked up to a ventilator wheeled up to me with a confident smile. I knew immediately who she was. The light in her eyes assured me this was the same young woman. She was happily headed for home and making the most of every day on the way."[6]

On her way to her heavenly home, that is. And along the way she had settled into a living situation with a friend and was attending college.

We might pause and ask ourselves what would have happened if Lisa had given up hope. What if she had succumbed to the seemingly infallible logic that her life had become worthless?

Unlike some of the stories we have learned about, Lisa did not experience physical healing, though she must have prayed for that also. The healing that she received was for the transformation of her mind and her spirit. And this is the more enduring healing, for our bodies will one day pass away.

With her newfound optimism and zest for life, the young quadriplegic Lisa has undoubtedly touched many

> *S*he reminded her that paraplegics have one great advantage in that they can more easily obey the command: "Be still, and know that I am God."
>
> *Psalm 46:10*

Healing Through the Power of Prayer

lives that would not have been touched otherwise.

And this is part of the mystery of the Divine. We have heard the stories of those who have received dramatic physical healing, which is a cause of great rejoicing. Others have not been healed completely, yet they saw the skillful transforming work of the Great Physician in bringing needed change into their lives. Still others have traversed the valley of great loss and have emerged with a profound depth and richness of spirit. And then there are those, like Joni and Lisa, who live lives of handicap and pain, but whose inner lives shine like precious gemstones.

Few of us would choose any of this. We want the best of all possible worlds in which our prayers are promptly answered so that we are spared any pain. But our Creator has far better things in store for us, as expressed in the prayer of an unknown Confederate soldier: "I asked for strength that I might achieve; I was made weak that I might learn humbly to obey. I asked for health that I might do greater things; I was given infirmity that I might do better things.

The healing that she received was for the transformation of her mind and her spirit. And this is the more enduring healing, for our bodies will one day pass away.

Healing Through the Power of Prayer

I asked for riches that I might
    be happy;
  I was given poverty that I
    might be wise.
I asked for power that I might
    have the praise of men;
  I was given weakness that I
    might feel the need of God.

I asked for all things that I
    might enjoy life;
  I was given life that I might
    enjoy all things.
I got nothing that I had asked
    for,
  but everything that I had
    hoped for."[7]

PRAYERS
FOR HEALING

Jesus answered them, "Have faith in God. Truly I tell you, if you say to this mountain, 'Be taken up and thrown into the sea,' and if you do not doubt in your heart, but believe that what you say will come to pass, it will be done for you. So I tell you, whatever you ask for in prayer, believe that you have received it, and it will be yours."

Mark 11:22–24

Dear God,

You have been around since
    time began.
Help me to know that my life is
    important to you, that my
    health and well-being
    are important to you.
Just as Jesus restored sight
    to the blind, give me eyes
    to see your will in my life.
Heal me of my illnesses,
    my selfishness, my injuries.
Give me your peace.

                                    Amen

Healing Through the Power of Prayer

Dear God,

Help my unbelief.
When I'm in pain, I forget that you
  care about me.
I forget that you have helped me
  through my trials.
I forget that you hold me in your
  arms to keep me safe.
I forget that you are feeling
  my pain with me.
I forget that you love me.
I forget that I am important to you.
Show me your presence—let me feel
  your enveloping love.
Heal my hurting soul.
Thank you for staying with me even
  in my unbelief.

Amen

Dear God,

My body is still sick.
Why? Help me accept your will.
If I must be sick of body,
    please heal my soul, my heart,
    and my pain.
Show me your strength, that I
    may be strong.
Hold me in your hands,
    that I may rest knowing your
    presence.
Help me accept what is in store
    for my body.
Let your peace flood my soul.

                              Amen

Healing Through the Power of Prayer

Endnotes

Part I: A Brief History of Healing

Chapter 1: The Miracle Kid

1. As told by Jan Goodwin in "The Miracle Kid," *Family Circle*, January 9, 1996, p. 82.

2. Claudia Wallis, "Faith and Healing," *Time*, June 24, 1996, p. 64.

3. Sharon Doyle Driedger, "Prayer Power," *Maclean's*, September 25, 1995, p. 42.

4. Ibid.

5. Tom Harpur, *The Uncommon Touch: An Investigation Into Spiritual Healing* (Toronto: McClelland & Stewart, Inc., 1994), pp. 26–27.

6. Ibid., p. 30.

7. Ibid., p. 32.

8. Joan Borysenko and Miroslav Borysenko, *The Power of the Mind to Heal* (Carson, California: Hay House, 1994), p. 2.

9. Ibid., p. 24.

10. Ibid., p. 26.

11. Ibid., p. 10.

12. Blair Justice, *Who Gets Sick: How Beliefs, Moods, and Thoughts Affect Your Health* (Los Angeles: Jeremy P. Tarcher, Inc., 1988), p. 292.

13. Goodwin, ibid.

14. Harpur, pp. 26–27.

15. Morton Kelsey, *Healing and Christianity* (Minneapolis: Augsburg, 1995), p. 267; emphasis added.

16. David B. Larson and Mary A. Greenwold Milano, "Are Religion and Spirituality Relevant in Health Care?" *Mind/Body Medicine* 1, no. 3 (1995): pp. 147–57; quoted in Larry Dossey, *Prayer Is Good Medicine* (San Francisco: HarperSanFrancisco, 1996), p. 3.

17. Wallis, p. 60.

Chapter 2: Let This Tumor Wither!

1. Benedict Heron, *Channels of Healing Prayer* (Notre Dame, Indiana: Ave Maria Press, 1989), p. 18.

2. Ibid.

3. Francis MacNutt, *Healing* (Notre Dame: Ave Maria Press, 1974), p. 245; quoted in Kenneth L. Bakken and Kathleen H. Hofeller, *The Journey Toward Wholeness: A Christ-Centered Approach to Health and Healing* (New York: Crossroad, 1992), p. 84.

4. *The Book of Common Prayer.* According to the Use of the Anglican Church of England. Oxford: The University Press, 1970; quoted in Kelsey, p. 13.

5. Kelsey, pp. 315–316.

6. Kelsey, p. 17.

7. Wade H. Boggs, Jr., *Faith Healing & The Christian Faith* (Richmond, Virginia: John Knox Press, 1956), p. 17; referenced in Kelsey, pp. 19-20.

Chapter 4:
Jesus' Healing Ministry

1. Kelsey, p. 63.

Chapter 5:
Healing Through the Ages

1. Saint Augustine, *The City of God* XXII.8 (1954); p. 445; quoted in Kelsey, p. 146.

2. *City of God* XXII.8 (1954), p. 450; quoted in Kelsey, p. 147.

3. Saint Augustine, *Retractationum* I.13.7, in *Patrologiae Latginae* 32 (1877), cols. 604–605; quoted in Kelsey, p. 146.

4. See Kelsey, pp. 146–149; Evelyn Frost, *Christian Healing* (London: A. R. Mowbray, 1940).

5. Justin Martyr, *Second Apology: To the Roman Senate*, p. 6; quoted in Kelsey, p. 108.

6. Ibid.

7. Sulpitius Severus, *Life of St. Martin* VII; quoted in Kelsey, p. 150.

8. Gregory the Great, *The Book of Pastoral Rule* II.13; quoted in Kelsey, p. 154.

9. Quoted in Kelsey, p. 166.

10. Barbara Tuchman, *A Distant Mirror: The Calamitous Fourteenth Century* (New York: Ballantine Books, 1978), p. 104; quoted in Bakken and Hofeller, p. 21.

Chapter 6:
There's No Turning Back!

1. *The Unlimited Power of Prayer* (Garden City: Doubleday & Company, Inc., 1982), p. 107.

2. Ibid., p. 108.

3. Ibid., p. 109.

Part II:
Why Do Bad Things Happen?

Chapter 7:
The Sources of Sickness

1. David Spiegel, "A Psychosocial Intervention and Survival Time of Patients with Metastatic Breast Cancer," *Advances* 7, no. 3 (Summer 1991): pp. 10–19; quoted in Larry Dossey, *Healing Words: The Power of Prayer and the Practice of Medicine* (San Francisco: Harper, 1993), p. 58.

2. Dossey, *Prayer Is Good Medicine*, p. 158.

3. Spiegel, "A Psychosocial Intervention," p. 15; quoted in Dossey, *Healing Words*, p. 58.

4. Borysenko and Borysenko, p. 71.

5. Dossey, *Healing Words*, p. 57.

6. Ibid., p. 58.

7. Harpur, pp. 237–238.

8. Ibid.

9. Harold S. Kushner, *When Bad Things Happen to Good People* (New York: Avon Books, 1981), p. 45.

10. Ibid., 129.

Chapter 8:
The Sources of Sickness II

1. Kelsey, p. 74n.

2. Kushner, p. 22.

3. Kelsey, p. 75.

4. Ibid., pp. 75–76.

5. Quoted in Heron, p. 87.

6. Kushner, p. 10.

Part III:
How to Pray for Healing

Chapter 9:
A Tale of Two Villages

1. Heron, p. 65.

2. Ibid., p. 62.

3. Ibid.

4. Harpur, pp. 194–195.

5. Ibid.

6. Heron, pp. 13–14.

7. Ibid., p. 36.

Chapter 10:
The Importance of Faith

1. Heron, p. 52.

2. Bakken and Hofeller, pp. 69–70.

3. Heron, p. 50.

Chapter 11:
Miracle Workers

1. Bert Ghezzi, *Miracles of the Saints: A Book of Reflections* (Grand Rapids, Michigan: Zondervan, 1996), p. 41.

2. Ibid., p. 42.

3. Ibid., p. 44.

4. Heron, p. 43.

5. Ibid., pp. 23–24.

6. Ibid.

7. Ibid., p. 25.

8. Ibid., p. 24.

9. Ibid., p. 123.

10. Ibid., p. 53.

11. Ibid., p. 124.

Chapter 12:
Healing Places

1. Joe Nickell, *Looking for a Miracle* (Amherst, New York: Prometheus Books, 1993), p. 151.

2. Heron, p. 143.

3. Ibid.

4. Kelsey, p. 232.

Part IV:
When Healing Doesn't Come

Chapter 13:
The Power of Forgiveness

1. Harpur, p. 157.

2. Lewis B. Smedes, *Forgive and Forget: Healing the Hurts We Don't Deserve* (San Francisco: Harper & Row, 1984), pp. 126–127.

3. Ibid., p. 127.

4. Ibid.

5. Ibid., pp. 119–120.

6. Ibid., p. 120.

7. Ibid., p. 29.

8. Ibid., p. 95.

9. Greg Anderson, *The Triumphant Patient* (Nashville: Thomas Nelson Publishers, 1992), p. 81.

10. Dan B. Allender and Tremper Longman III, *The Cry of the Soul: How Our Emotions Reveal Our Deepest Questions About God* (Colorado Springs, Colorado: NavPress, 1994), pp. 149–150.

11. Smedes, pp. 86–87.

12. Bridget Mary Meehan, *The Healing Power of Prayer* (Liguori, Missouri: Liguori Publications, 1988), pp. 61–62.

13. Kelsey, p. 295.

14. Heron, p. 70.

15. Ibid., p. 81.

Chapter 14:
Wrong Motives

1. Dossey, *Prayer*, p. 95.

2. Ibid.

3. Bakken and Hofeller, p. 102.

4. Kelsey, p. 221.

Chapter 15:
A Thorn in the Flesh

1. Meehan, p. 35.

2. Ibid., p. 36.

Part V:
The Big Picture

Chapter 16:
Through the Valley

1. Marjorie Holmes, *To Help You Through the Hurting* (Garden City, New York: Doubleday, 1983), p. 55.

2. Ibid., p. 55.

3. Ibid. p. 55–56.

4. Roberta Andresen, "The Best Thing That Ever Happened to Me," in Jack Canfield, Mark Victor Hansen, Patty Aubery, Nancy Mitchell, *Chicken Soup for the Surviving Soul* (Deerfield Beach, Florida: Health Communications, 1996), p. 322.

5. Ibid.

6. Ibid., p. 323.

Chapter 17:
The Way Home

1. Joni Eareckson Tada, *Heaven—Your Real Home* (Grand Rapids, Michigan: Zondervan, 1995), p. 29.

2. Ibid., p. 176.

3. Ibid., p. 39.

4. Ibid., p. 187.

5. Ibid., p. 189.

6. Ibid., p. 193.

7. George Appleton, ed., *The Oxford Book of Prayer* (Oxford: Oxford University Press, 1985), p. 119.

Index

Healing, Christian. *See also* Healing
  ministries of Jesus; Miracles.
  anointing with oil, 64–65,
    166–173
  corporate (group) prayer, 10–11,
    67
  early church, 71–72, 73–74
  history, 70–79
  holistic, 149–151, 181, 205
  importance of faith, 64–66,
    142–155
  laying on of hands, 62–63,
    170–173
  Middle Ages, 77–79
  modes, 135–139
  Paul's works, 215–216
  preventing further deterioration,
    136–137
  public request for, 168–169
  slain in the spirit, 202–204
  souls, 139, 239–240
  temporary, 138–139
Healing ministries of Jesus, 33,
    56–69. *See also* Miracles.
  blindness, 91–92, 130–131,
    147–148
  locations, 66–68
  methods, 62–64, 125–127
  paralyzation, 50–51
  people's responses, 59–61
  role in mission, 114
  Roman servant, 142–144
  Sabbath, 114
Heart disease. *See* Cardiovascular
    disease.
Hebrews, Book of, 66, 148
Herod the Great, 90
Heron, Benedict (Father)
  arresting sickness, 136
  dying peacefully, 141
  faith and medical care, 38–39
  gradual healing, 136

Heron, Benedict (Father) (continued)
  importance of humility, 205
  praying authentically, 165–166
  slain in the spirit, 202–204
Hezekiah, 64, 138, 152–153
Hofeller, Kathleen, 149, 211
Holistic healing, 149–151, 181, 205
Holmes, Marjorie, 226
Hope, 102, 228–230
Hufford, David J., 20–21
Hughes, Harold, 80–87
Humility, 205, 218–219
Huxley, Aldous, 208–209

I
International Medical Commission,
    177, 179
Isaiah, prophecy of, 56–58

J
James, Book of
  anointing with oil, 166–167, 168
  importance of faith, 64–65
  prayers for healing, 48–49
  trust in God, 144–145
  unanswered prayers, 209
Jerusalem, 50, 90–91
Jessudas, M., 171–173
Jesus. *See also* Healing ministries of
    Jesus; Miracles.
  embodiment of, 53–54
  forgiveness of enemies, 185–187,
    188–189
  mission, 56–58, 114, 144, 206
  resurrection, 229
Job, Book of, 43, 108
John, Gospel of
  Kingdom of God, 57
  Pool of Bethesda, 175
  power of evil, 110–111
  purpose of blindness, 91
  view of body, 54

Healing Through the Power of Prayer

Healing Through the Power of Prayer